Cryptocurrency Trading Strategies For Beginners: 50+ Tips& Secrets For Day Trading Bitcoin+ Alt Coins, Market Psychology, Technical Analysis& Making A Living In Crypto

By Brandon Smith

Preface

Unless you are under a rock since the beginning of this year, you would have definitely heard about cryptos loud and clear. 2021 has undoubtfully been the best year for crypto since the past ten years. The level of impact created by cryptos in less than a decade of their inception is unmatchable. Individuals from various disciplines are watching the crypto space with a lot of interest and this population is not just confined to people in the world of finance. It is not a surprise to see a statistic that say cryptos are among the most spoken topics in the previous decade.

There are numerous speculations in this area right from the start. Many experts put forward their opinion on cryptos that it could change the face of economies in the ways we can't imagine. A few of them believed that this global crypto phenomenon is a bubble that may burst anytime. The latter opinion is ultimately proven wrong as the crypto industry is stronger than ever today with more than $1.7 trillion is market capitalization.

This industry has made more millionaires in a shorter period than any other industry in the world. Many of the individuals are generating a constant stream of passive income from cryptos by investing, trading, and mining them. We will be discussing each of these topics in various sections of this book. According to market experts, most of the cryptos in the market are still undervalued as per their fundamental & technical analysis.

Therefore, this is the right time for us to identify & invest in those cryptos with strong fundamentals but are undervalued. Investing in them now is one of the best financial decisions you can ever take as they may reap huge profits for us in the near future. But as a matter of fact, education is crucial before investing or trading anything that we aren't completely aware of. The fundamental purpose of this book is to give you that basic yet essential education in the simplest way possible.

The most powerful aspect of this book is the integration of various trading strategies that are used across the industries and apply them for crypto.

By learning those strategies and applying them on the real markets, you can exponentially increase your profits as they are rigorously back tested. Excited much? Let's get started!

Disclaimer

Please do consider using this e-book only for directional purposes and not as an ultimate guide. All the content provided in this book are as accurate as per the time of writing. But there might be some minor errors in content or typography. Therefore, use this guide with the utmost care and cross-check the facts before making any investment or trading decision.

This book is curated by professional authors who have a lot of experience in the crypto field. They could have got this information from various sources or their own experience. That doesn't mean their predictions can't go wrong. Also, this guide links to various investments and related financial products that the authors have used before.

The ideas/suggestions provided by the authors in this book are simply the ones that have worked for them before. They make no claims that these suggestions will work no matter what. So please be careful before making any real investments and verify the actualities before making decisions. Always remember that due diligence is crucial while making investments in crypto space.

Both the author and the publisher hold no responsibility for the funds you are going to invest and the losses that you may incur. The whole purpose of this guide is to educate and direct you on the right path while making investment decisions. We hold no responsibility or liability to any individual or entity concerning any damage or loss caused or alleged to be caused directly or indirectly by this e-book.

Table of Contents

Session 1
Introduction to
Cryptocurrency

1.1 What is Cryptocurrency?

A cryptocurrency is a decentralized digital currency based on blockchain technology. The defining security feature of a cryptocurrency is cryptography — hence the name crypto makes counterfeiting or double-spending impossible. Since cryptocurrencies are decentralized, it means that they are not issued nor under the control of any government, or any individual for that matter. This is made possible by blockchain technology which works as a distributed ledger stored across a network of user computers globally.

Let's now understand some of the crypto terms and jargon you must know before going further.

Altcoins - Before we delve deeper into cryptocurrencies, you should first understand the different types of cryptocurrencies. Altcoins represents all other cryptocurrencies except Bitcoin.

Security Tokens - These are altcoins that pay dividends or make the holder a shareholder in a business venture. They are traded the same way stocks are traded in stock exchanges. These coins are subject to strict regulations under securities laws. These cryptocurrencies are typically issued in an initial coin offering (ICO).

Stablecoins - These are cryptocurrencies whose value depends on an underlying asset. Their value can be based on other fiat currencies or other cryptocurrencies. These are called fiat-collateralized and crypto-collateralized coins, respectively. Non-collateralized stable coins derive their value from algorithms that adjust the supply of the crypto based on demand.

Mining-Based Altcoins - These are altcoins that have a similar mining process to Bitcoin.

Utility Tokens - These cryptocurrencies allow the holder to access a company's products or services. It also allows them privileges than they would otherwise not receive if they didn't own the utility tokens. Such privileges include special discounts or are the first in line to sample new products. These altcoins are not subjected to rigorous scrutiny by security laws like security altcoins.

1.2 How does Cryptocurrency Work?

Originally, cryptocurrencies were designed to be a digital currency that facilitated transactions online, anonymously. However, the functions of cryptocurrencies have since morphed, and they now serve various purposes. This section will discuss; how you can send and receive cryptocurrencies, how you can store them, how to buy them with fiat money, and how the cryptocurrency network is supported.

Buying Cryptocurrency

Before you buy a cryptocurrency, here are a few steps you should consider:

1. Decide which Cryptocurrency you want to buy. There are over 5000 cryptocurrencies in the market; you should select ones that suit your transactions or investment needs.

2. The purpose of buying cryptocurrencies: as we mentioned earlier, cryptocurrencies have several purposes. We will discuss them in a later section. If you intend on speculatively trading cryptocurrencies, you may prefer

looking into crypto derivatives such as exchange-traded funds and CFDs – we explain these in Session 4. However, if you intend to use Cryptocurrency for transactional purposes, you will have to buy the actual crypto.

3. Where to buy Cryptocurrency: there are several websites to buy cryptocurrencies. However, we advise purchasing cryptocurrencies from reputable crypto exchanges to avoid being scammed. Here are some factors to consider when selecting where to buy cryptocurrencies:

- Security of the platform to ensure that you do not lose your cryptos to hackers
- The number of cryptocurrencies available, just in case you'd want to diversify your crypto portfolio in the future.
- The average time it takes for your account to be activated.
- Also, make sure to check user reviews. This will give you first-hand insight from users of the platform.

4. The cost of buying the Cryptocurrency: before you sign up with a crypto exchange to buy cryptocurrencies, you must first acquaint yourself with the fees they charge. Some crypto exchanges charge exorbitant fees, making the cost of a cryptocurrency significantly higher than the market price. Compare the cost from a few exchanges before settling on one.

5. Regulatory restrictions: some crypto exchanges have been banned in some countries. So, make sure to confirm that your country allows your preferred crypto exchange. Note that you may use virtual private networks (VPNs) to bypass such restrictions.

6. Check the payment methods available. You should also consider the acceptable modes of payment available in your preferred crypto exchange. Different exchanges accept different payment methods such as bank transfer, credit and debit cards, online payments like PayPal, and even cash.

After you have completed this checklist, create an account with your preferred crypto exchange. Typically, the steps for creating an account are fairly standard, and it should averagely take five minutes. After your account has been fully verified, you can deposit funds with your credit or debit card via bank transfer, PayPal, or other methods available from the crypto exchange.

You can also buy Cryptocurrency directly from other people. This is called peer-to-peer exchange – there are no intermediaries. However, you need to create an account with an exchange that facilitates peer-to-peer exchange.

Cryptocurrency ATMs: You can also buy cryptocurrencies at physical ATMs. Unlike the conventional ATMs, where you can deposit and withdraw fiat currencies, crypto ATMs allow you to buy cryptocurrencies and store them in your cryptocurrency wallet anonymously. You have to physically be present at these crypto ATMs to buy the Cryptocurrency. Unlike online exchanges, crypto ATMs provide very limited types of cryptocurrencies that you can buy. Note that you must have a crypto wallet for you to buy cryptocurrencies at the ATM. You simply input your cryptocurrency wallet address, then deposit money into the ATM, and the ATM sends cryptos to your wallet. Sometimes if you don't have a wallet, the ATM will create one for you.

Cryptocurrency Wallet: When you buy cryptocurrencies, you store them in a crypto wallet. A cryptocurrency wallet is a program that allows you to receive, send, and store cryptocurrencies. There are several types of cryptocurrency wallets. Some of them include desktop, mobile, online, hardware, and paper crypto wallets. Cryptocurrency wallets have both private and public keys.

Public key: is a long alphanumeric sequence which is your wallet's address. This is the address that people use to send cryptocurrencies to you. Think of it as your bank account number, which you can give to anyone to send or deposit money into your account.

Private key: is what you use to access the Cryptocurrency stored in your wallet. It is like the PIN to your bank account, which you should keep secret. Note that not all wallets give you sole control of your private keys, which means you do not explicitly control the cryptos in your wallet.

Note: We will extensively discuss cryptocurrency wallets in 'Session 4'.

Sending and Receiving Cryptocurrency

For you to send or receive cryptocurrencies, you must have a cryptocurrency wallet. To receive cryptos, you must give the sender your public key, and you must have their public key to send them cryptos. Sometimes the steps involved in sending and receiving cryptocurrencies may differ depending on the wallet or the type of Cryptocurrency. Here are the general steps that you will follow.

Keep in mind that you can only send and receive like-coins. This means that if you have a Bitcoin wallet, you can only send or receive Bitcoin.

1. Log into your crypto wallet
2. Go to the "Send/Receive" screen, ideally by clicking on the proper tab
3. If you are sending cryptos, input the recipient's public key, then enter the amount

you wish to send. To avoid sending cryptos to the wrong address, it is advisable to copy and paste the address to minimize typos. After you have confirmed you have the right address, you can complete the transaction. Alternatively, you can scan a QR code of the recipient's address, which eliminates typo mistakes.

4. To receive cryptocurrencies into your wallet, you need to share your public address with the sender.

What is Blockchain?

This is the technology upon which cryptocurrencies are built. Any cryptocurrency transaction is recorded in "blocks" and is linked to a previous crypto transaction, i.e., "chained". These transactions are stored in various computers and are updated simultaneously as new transactions happen. This ensures that all records are identical and accurate and that no one person can alter them.

Typically, transaction verification is done using either of two validation techniques: proof of work (PoW) or proof of stake (PoS). Without these validation techniques, the decentralization aspect of cryptocurrencies would collapse.

Proof of work: It is a consensus algorithm used to verify transactions on a blockchain. The PoW is designed to prevent 51% attack also known as double-spends. Cryptocurrencies use the PoW consensus method to validate a particular transaction and produce new blocks added to the chain. This is the oldest consensus method and also among the most popular algorithms.

Note that the blockchain network requires that users maintain the integrity of the network – a process called mining. With PoW, crypto miners are responsible for completing the transactions on the network and are rewarded for their accuracy and speed.

In PoW, computers in the network are miners. These miners have to solve complex mathematical equations to verify transactions. Typically, the first miner to solve these equations is the one that gets a reward –

usually in crypto. Naturally, this mining process requires a lot of computing power and consumes a lot of electricity. In practice, most miners may incur higher costs than the rewards they receive.

The mathematical equations that need to be solved range from Byzantine generic problems to the intricate hashing function. The hash function is a process of generating a randomized output using an input of a specific length. In this case, the hash is the determinant of who mines the block accurately – it is a numerical value.

Miners also have to solve integer factorization, which involves decomposing a composite number into smaller integers alongside multiplications and prime number restrictions. This is a contingency puzzle protocol meant to safeguard the network against a DoS attack.

Proof of Stake: Unlike PoW, it doesn't need miners to solve a complex mathematical equation. Instead, the mining process depends on how much cryptos the miner has. Thus, the more cryptos one holds, the more mining power they have. Here's how it works.

Crypto holders stake their coins to allow them to participate in the validation process in a network. These coins are held in an escrow account. The staker then gets the opportunity to form the next block in the blockchain. This block is then verified by other nodes called endorsers. Note that the staker is the validator and is the one who gets rewarded if the block is correct.

When a node wants to become a validator, they stake their coins. The selection process can either be a randomized block selection or a coin age selection.

Randomized block selection involves selecting the node with the highest stake and the lowest number of hashes.

The coin age selection involves selecting the node which has staked their cryptos for the longest period to form the next block. It presumes that this node has been honest and dedicated for the longest time.

Note that proof of stake has a few protocols. They include Delegated Proof-of-Stake (DPoS), Delegated Proof-of-Contribution (DPoC), Liquid Proof-of-Stake (LPoS), Hybrid Proof-of-Stake (HPoS), and Pure Proof-of-Stake (PPoS).

Advantages of Proof of Stake over Proof of Work

Proof of Stake consensus was devised as a replacement for Proof of Work which has become increasingly inefficient and unscalable. Here are some advantages of PoS over PoW.

1. The cost of mining with PoS is much lower than PoW. That is because PoS doesn't burn electricity like PoW. Miners don't need powerful mining computers. This significantly lowers the cost of mining which means that miners get to be profitable.

2. PoS is arguably more decentralized than PoW. As we've mentioned, PoW miners need powerful computers. This means that significant crypto mining operations have been confined to very few large-scale operators, making cryptos mined through

PoW a little less decentralized. In PoS, anyone with cryptos can be a staker.

3. PoW has a higher chance of a 51% attack compared to PoS. This could occur if there is cooperation among large-scale miners to create fraudulent transaction blocks. In PoS, since you must own the crypto to be a miner, it wouldn't be in your best interest to attack the network since you will be the biggest loser.

1.3 What Makes Cryptocurrencies Different from Traditional Currencies?

Cryptocurrencies are touted as the future of money. Crypto enthusiasts maintain that cryptos will eventually edge out fiat money. Naturally, this is because they believe that cryptos fix the fundamental flaws inherent in fiat currencies. So, what makes cryptos different from traditional currencies? Here are the reasons:

Cryptocurrencies are Decentralized

As we have mentioned throughout this book, cryptocurrencies are decentralized. It means that they are not issued by a central authority nor its circulation controlled by the issuing entity. Decentralization in cryptocurrencies is achieved through blockchain technology, where users worldwide who are on the crypto network verify transactions and create new blocks. This way, no single individual controls what happens on the network.

Fiat currencies are issued and controlled by central banks. Central banks decide what currency denominations are in circulation to withdraw a particular denomination through demonetization. More so, the government and central banks can decide to control the amount of money in circulation and its value through monetary and fiscal policies.

Some might argue that fiat money can also be digitized. They can be, but not the way cryptocurrencies are. Cryptocurrencies are based on blockchain technology, while digitizing fiat currencies would require them to be backed by physical money deposited at the bank.

Cryptocurrencies are Finite

Cryptocurrencies are limited in supply. For example, the maximum number of Bitcoins is 21 million. This means that when the number of Bitcoins in circulation reaches 21 million, no more Bitcoins will be mined. More so, the process of mining is very slow since it involves solving complex cryptographic equations. Thus, you cannot expect that a miner mines 1 million coins, then the one million coins will be added to the market overnight. How is limited supply achieved? Simple. Remember that cryptocurrencies are digital; there is no physical currency. This means

28

cryptocurrencies are just lines of codes. Within these codes, the supply of that crypto is written.

On the other hand, governments and central banks control the supply of money. They can arbitrarily decide to issue more money into the market. More so, they have several mechanisms aimed at controlling the supply of the currency in circulation. They decide whether to reduce or increase the supply of money in the economy. In recent times, quantitative easing (QE) has been the most popular. QE involves central banks purchasing bonds or other interest-bearing financial assets from the government. These bonds can just be created out of nowhere. By buying these bonds from the government, the central bank effectively increases the amount of money in circulation, that's why it's commonly referred to as printing money.

Central banks can also influence the supply of money by setting the reserve requirement. This is the amount of money that commercial banks are required to bank with the central bank. If the reserve requirement increases, the money supply in the economy drops; conversely, a decrease in the reserve requirement frees up more money for commercial banks to lend into the economy.

Similarly, central banks use interest rates to control the supply of money. Increasing interest rates encourages people to save and discourages borrowing from the economy, effectively reducing the money supply. Lowering interest rates encourages people to borrow from banks and discourages savings, effectively increasing the money supply.

In short, the supply of fiat currencies entirely depends on whether fiscal and monetary policies are expansionary or deflationary. The supply of cryptocurrencies is fixed and cannot be changed.

Cryptocurrencies are More Secure and Anonymous, unlike Fiat

Cryptocurrencies are encrypted cryptographically. Cryptographic encryption is designed to secure every transaction in the blockchain. This makes it impossible for someone to hack and steal your coins. When you sign up for a crypto wallet, you are provided with an alphanumeric public and private key. Although the public key is in the public domain on the network, no one will ever know it belongs to you unless you tell them. More so, you do not provide personal information such as your name, passport/identity card number, where you live, or photographic identity.

When you register for a bank account or a credit card, you are obligated to provide personally identifiable information. Every transaction into and out of your account is monitored and tracked. Combined with the fact that most banking cybersecurity is awfully vulnerable, both your money and personal data are unsafe. Remember that with cryptocurrencies, it is impossible for anyone to trace your transactions back to you – your real-world identity remains anonymous.

Cryptocurrencies are Transparent

Blockchain technology, upon which all cryptocurrencies are based, operates as a public ledger. Every transaction is public and cannot be altered. Remember that every transaction must be validated in blockchain and forms a new block in the network. Thus, every block is formed in chronological order, making it impossible for someone to go back and alter or forge a transaction. The verification process involves every user seeing and confirming a transaction. This means that every transaction on the blockchain is authenticated.

It is commonplace in the fiat monetary system for unscrupulous persons to backdate transactions or fraudulently forging bank slips and claim that a transaction was done. You can also send money and then contact your bank to reverse that transaction. With mobile banking, you can even do the reversal yourself. With cryptocurrencies, the transaction is irreversible! After a block is formed, that transaction is done. No one can reverse it. Not even Satoshi Nakamoto.

Cryptocurrencies are Fast and Global

When you send or receive cryptocurrencies, the transactions are propagated instantly within the network and take a couple of minutes to verify the transaction. Provided you have an internet connection, and you can send cryptos to anyone in any part of the world. Although globalization has made it possible to transfer fiat money worldwide, there is a lot of bureaucracy involved and limits on how much you can transfer via a specific means. Note that there is no limit to how much you can transfer with cryptocurrencies.

You also don't need permission from anyone to send cryptos to anyone. You must convert your fiat currency into another currency for you to spend it in another part of the world. This can be a slow and costly process. You must disclose your transaction and seek permission when transferring money beyond a specific limit.

Cryptocurrencies are not Susceptible to Inflation
The value of fiat currencies entirely depends on the rate of inflation. By definition, inflation occurs when the price of goods and services increases rapidly, making money lose its purchasing power. In an economy, inflation can be caused by increased demand for goods and services, an increase in money supply, an unsustainable increase in national debt, and an unsustainable increase in production cost.

However, an increase in money supply tends to be the most common cause of inflation, and as we've mentioned, governments and central banks can arbitrarily increase the supply of money, resulting in inflation. This makes the fiat currencies lose their value. Generally, the value of fiat currencies heavily depends on economic performance and policies within a country.

Cryptocurrencies, on the other hand, are decentralized and not impacted by such policies. The value of cryptocurrencies entirely depends on demand. Thus, when the demand for cryptocurrencies is high, their value increases.

1.4 Fundamental Properties of Cryptocurrencies

Cryptocurrencies are considered as both assets and medium of exchange. This means that they possess fundamental properties that allow them to be regarded as such. The fundamental properties of cryptocurrencies are:

Cryptocurrencies are Scarce

For anything to have value, it must be limited in supply; and cryptocurrencies are fundamental, limited in supply. Although the crypto mining process churns out new coins into the market, this process won't go on forever. That is because it is coded within the cryptocurrencies the maximum supply of the coins. For example, the maximum limit for Bitcoin is capped at 21 million. This means that once all 21 million Bitcoins have been mined, there will be no more coins added to the market.

Arguably, this scarcity property of cryptocurrencies makes them valuable. In fact, the value of cryptocurrencies entirely depends on their demand. The crypto mining process involves solving complex mathematical equations. Thus, new cryptos are added to the market at a slow pace, ensuring that the value of cryptos remains relatively stable over time. Unlike fiat currencies, governments and central banks might decide to pump trillions into the economy overnight.

This fundamental property of cryptocurrencies also makes them inflation-free. Cryptos are immune to inflation caused by an increase in the money supply.

Decentralized Blockchain

Decentralized is perhaps the most commonly used term when referring to cryptocurrencies. As used in cryptocurrencies, decentralized means that cryptocurrencies are not issued, not controlled by a single entity. The control of the blockchain network upon which cryptocurrencies are based is under the control of crypto users worldwide. That's because the network relies on these users to maintain its integrity and verify transactions. This means that no single individual can have undue influence over the system.

Blockchain technology ensures that transactions on a network are permanent and immutable. For someone to hack the blockchain network, they must control more than 51% of the network. This is impossible. It would require millions of users working in concert to achieve this. Effectively, Decentralization served to create trust among the users of cryptocurrencies and to empower them.

Cryptocurrencies are easily accessible

Either as an asset or a means of payment, cryptocurrencies are easily accessible. Anyone in any part of the world can buy cryptocurrencies and transfer them to anyone provided they have a crypto address. All one needs to do is have an internet connection to create a crypto address and sign up for an exchange where they can buy cryptocurrencies or have someone send them some. This entire process is relatively easy and takes less than five minutes on average.

More so, you can easily convert cryptos to fiat currencies or other cryptos. Thus, holding cryptocurrencies is not an inconvenience in any form. It is for this reason that other assets are not used as a means of exchange payment. For example, precious metals are valuable and scarce, just like cryptocurrencies, but they are not easily accessible.

Cryptocurrencies are Widely Accepted

When cryptocurrencies were still at a nascent stage, not many people or businesses would accept them as payment or investment assets. However, with the increased mainstream adoption and regulations surrounding cryptocurrencies, they are becoming accepted universally. Businesses now accept payment in crypto, and mainstream exchanges have listed cryptocurrencies as tradable assets. Investment professionals, financial institutions, companies, and even government agencies have taken on cryptocurrencies as assets on the balance sheets.

We should note that cryptocurrencies tend to be volatile than fiat currencies. Until the volatility issues inherent in most cryptocurrencies are solved, they may not rise to a level where they entirely replace fiat currencies as the main form of exchange. However, stablecoins attempt to solve this.

Cryptocurrencies are divisible into smaller units

One fundamental property of any means of exchange is that it can be divided into smaller units. It would be impossible to use cryptocurrencies in transactions if they could not be divided into smaller units. This is meant to ensure that anyone can use them in a transaction. For example, as of this publication, the price of one Bitcoin is $47,274. One Bitcoin can be divisible by eight decimal places to the smallest unit called the Satoshi.

Thus, 1 Satoshi = 0.00000001 BTC, i.e., hundredth of a millionth Bitcoin.

If it were not divisible, it would be impossible for anyone with less than that amount to use Bitcoin for investment or transactional purposes. This is also why precious metals are not used for transactional purposes since they are not divisible.

Session 2
Brief History

2.1 Origin of Bitcoin

Before the creation of Bitcoin in 2008, there were several attempts at creating digital cash. In 1992, the idea of using computational puzzles to create value was discussed by two cryptographers - Cynthia Dwork and Moni Naor. In 1997, the first spam control proof-of-work scheme was used to develop hashcash, a system designed to reduce email spams and DoS attacks. But the first real concept of cryptocurrency was first discussed in 1998 by Wei Dai and Nick Szabo on the Cypherpunks mailing list. This was the first mention of digital currency, which uses cryptography to control its creation and transactions instead of a central authority. In 2005, Nick Szabo proposed the creation of 'bitgold', which would have been decentralized and adopt a blockchain-like system.

Bitgold did not catch on since it could not solve the double-spending problem. In bitgold's case, a user could copy and paste the digital token and continue spending it in perpetuity. Although the concept of bitgold failed, many crypto enthusiasts maintain that it gave birth to the creation of Bitcoin.

However, Bitcoin's journey started with the publication of a white paper – "Bitcoin: A Peer-to-Peer Electronic Cash System" – on October 31, 2008, by Satoshi Nakamoto. This whitepaper described what Bitcoin is and effectively solved the double-spending problem that plagued bitgold by deploying a decentralized system. The first Bitcoin block was mined on January 3, 2009. It is commonly referred to as Block 0, called the 'genesis block' and contains the text "The Times 03/Jan/2009 Chancellor on the brink of second bailout for banks". This comment is famously from the British newspaper 'The Times' and is seen as proof of the date when the first Bitcoin was mined.

Based on the comment attached to the genesis block, it can be argued that the financial crisis of 2008 precipitated the creation of Bitcoin. It wasn't until January 8, 2009, when the first version of Bitcoin, version 0.1, was released on the Cryptography Mailing list.

Satoshi Nakamoto made Bitcoin's source code open to the public and encouraged other cryptographers to continue developing Bitcoin. Ever since the first block was mined, Bitcoin mining has continued in earnest, encouraging the development of thousands of altcoins.

The first known exchange rate for Bitcoin was established in October 2009, where the US $1 was equivalent to 1309.03 BTC. This exchange was a derivative of the cost incurred to mined Bitcoins. It wasn't until February 2011 when Bitcoin achieved parity with the US dollar, i.e., 1BTC = $1.

The first known commercial transaction using Bitcoin, and perhaps a major milestone for the cryptocurrency, was on May 22, 2010, when 10000 BTC was used to purchase pizza.

2.2 Significant Cryptocurrencies in The Market

After the creation of Bitcoin and proving its value, several other cryptocurrencies emerged. There are more than 5000 known cryptocurrencies in circulation today, with many more being created.

The term altcoin is used to refer to cryptocurrencies that are not Bitcoin. We will discuss some of the most notable altcoins in the market. Our ranking of the most notable cryptocurrencies is based on their market capitalization and the 24-hour tradable volume. These two factors may accurately be used to determine their popularity.

However, note that the value of cryptocurrencies depends on the demand they have in the market. Therefore, it is entirely possible that a not-so-popular cryptocurrency might, in the near future, become one of the most popular crypto with a significant market share. Note that any data included here is as of February 2021.

Ethereum - It is a smart crypto platform that is decentralized and is the second most popular, just behind Bitcoin. The popularity of Ethereum stems from the fact that any decentralized offering can be built on the platform, the popular of which is decentralized Finance (DeFi). It is impossible to talk about Ethereum without mentioning DeFi.

ETH was proposed by Vitalik Buterin in 2013, followed by an overwhelming pre-launch ICO in 2014, with its initial release on July 30, 2015. It was primarily created to address Bitcoin's shortcoming, which, although popular, is limited in functionality. One can only send, receive, and perform basic transactions with Bitcoin. Ethereum strove to revolutionize financial services by the introduction of smart contracts. Ethereum argues that the platform can be used to decentralize, codify, trade and secure anything.

It gave birth to DeFi by supporting smart contracts and Decentralized Applications (DApps). With these two, anyone, anywhere, could create decentralized financial products and deploy them globally for free.

This is the driving force behind the popularity of Ethereum. Evidently, the implications of this are infinite, given that it eliminates the restrictions imposed by the centralized financial system.

Smart contracts used in Ethereum refer to contracts that automatically execute when the terms agreed upon by the parties are attained. Unlike conventional contracts whose execution depends on counterparties and including a third party, the agreement terms in smart contracts are written within lines of codes. In this case, the contract executes itself, with the transaction being irreversible and transparent for all parties. Note that, as is with anything on a blockchain network, the smart contract is decentralized. The most notable achievement of smart contracts is to enforce trust between anonymous parties eliminating the need for external enforcement mechanisms, legal systems, or central authority.

As of February 2021, 114,868,941 ETH is in circulation with a market capitalization of about $175 billion and an average daily turnover of $26.3 billion.

In December 2020, Ethereum launched Ethereum 2.0, which served to replace the Proof-of-Work consensus mechanism with the Proof-of-Stake mechanism. The PoS network is more efficient than PoW since it increases the transaction speed on the network and is easily scalable. With the rise of DeFi, and Bitcoin losing its transactional status, Ethereum is poised to be at the heart of cryptos future.

Cardano (ADA) - The development of Cardano began in 2015 and was officially launched in 2017 by Charles Hoskinson, who was among the lead engineers of Ethereum. Fundamentally, Cardano employs Ouroboros proof-of-stake consensus mechanism. ADA is in direct competition with Ethereum in terms of functionality.

As of February 2021, Cardano had a market capitalization of $41.295 billion with 31,948,309,441 ADA coins in circulation. ADA was priced at $1.29 with an average daily turnover of $10.32 billion.

Binance Coin (BNB) - BNB is essentially a utility token designed to pay trading fees on Binance crypto exchange – it is the cryptocurrency that powers Binance exchange. Binance exchange was founded in 2017 by Changpeng Zhao, and BNB was launched in July 2017 through an ICO. Initially, BNB was based on the Ethereum chain but later migrated to the Binance chain.

As a utility token, users who use it on the Binance exchange are eligible for special discounts in fees incurred during trading, deposits, conversions, and withdrawals. When it was launched, BNB was worth ten cents, and as of February 2021, it was worth $252.44 with a market capitalization of about 39 billion. There are 154,532,785 BNB in circulation with a daily turnover of $4.96 billion. Note that BNB is not mineable.

Tether (USDT) - Tether is one of the original stable coins. As a stable coin, it is a fiat-collateralized altcoin whose value is pegged on the USD. Tether was designed to eliminate the volatility which plagues cryptos making them rather inefficient mediums of exchange. Since it is backed by the USD, USDT holds the USD in a ration of 1:1. This means that 1 USDT = $1. This characteristic makes USDT the perfect medium of exchange. It attracts crypto skeptics since they can enjoy all the benefits of cryptocurrencies, along with the relative stability of the US dollar.

It was launched in 2014 and described itself as a blockchain platform meant to facilitate the use of fiat digitally. As of February 2021, Tether had a market capitalization of about $35.08 billion with a daily turnover of about $96.64 billion.

Polkadot (DOT) - Polkadot was launched through an ICO in October 2017 and arguably one of the most complex cryptocurrencies in the market. It is the brainchild of Dr Gavin Wood – a former lead developer in Ethereum. It operates with the proof-of-stake consensus mechanism. Polkadot's protocols are designed to foster interoperability between other blockchains by connecting permissioned and permissionless blockchains, including oracles. The platforms strive to power an entirely decentralized internet by making it possible for blockchains to exchange information. It is scalable and can be upgraded with these protocols being governed by DOT holders.

Just like ETH, DOT supports the creation of smart contracts and cryptos. Here's how the two differ. Developers on Polkadot are free to create their own blockchains but can also use Polkadot's security powered by its Relay Chain. This is what facilitates the interoperability of different networks. Unlike in Ethereum, developers can create new blockchains and create their own security measures, making smaller projects vulnerable to attacks.

As of February 2021, there were 914,414,277 DOT in circulation with a market capitalization of about $32.2 billion. The price of DOT was $35.21, with an average daily turnover of $3.36 billion. Polkadot is not minable.

Ripple XRP - Ripple's development began way back in the 2000s but was officially launched in 2012. Technically, Ripple refers to RippleNet, the platform which facilitates institutional asset exchange and a vast payment network for international monetary settlements. XRP is Ripple's native currency. XRP was dubbed "a banker's crypto" since it was designed for fiat as well as crypto transactions between institutions.

Ripple collaborates with over 40 global financial institutions, including Union Credit, UBC, and MoneyGram. Most transactions on RippleNet do not involve XRP, as institutions send fiat currencies across the network. In February 2021, XRP had a market capitalization of about $20.18 billion priced at $0.4444 and a daily turnover of $3.67 billion. Note that XRP is not minable.

Chainlink (LINK) - Chainlink is a secure "middleware" blockchain platform designed to facilitate the connection between smart contracts and data outside the blockchain network. It is a decentralized oracle network whose design was specifically for optimizing and popularizing smart contracts by eliminating inefficiencies and inaccuracies. The decentralized oracles on Chainlink enable the smart contracts to access data in the real world which Ethereum would otherwise not be able to. Note that Chainlink supports all types of blockchains.

While the platform provides a secure external connection, LINK is the token native to the network.

LINK was launched through an ICO in 2017 for $0.11. As of February 2021, it had a market capitalization of about $12.14 billion with a little over 410 million coins in circulation priced at $29.76. It had an average daily turnover of $2.93 billion. LINK is not mineable.

Litecoin (LTC) - Litecoin was released on October 7, 2011, by Charlie Lee. It was the first cryptocurrency to be launched after the launch of Bitcoin in 2008 and uses "Scrypt" as a Proof-of-Work consensus mechanism. Originally, LTC was designed to be an improved version of BTC — and in some ways, it was. The transaction costs on the LTC network are lower than BTC, and it takes roughly 2.5 minutes to process a block while Bitcoin processes a block in 10 minutes. The faster rate at which LTC blocks are generated means that it can accommodate more transactions at a higher transaction throughput.

As of February 2021, LTC had a market capitalization of about $11.97 billion with 66.58 billion LTC in circulation, each priced at $179.83. It had an average daily turnover of $4.82 billion.

Bitcoin Cash (BCH) - BCH was a result of a fork from Bitcoin. This is basically a division resulting from the blockchain creating two separate versions of the same cryptocurrency. BCH was created in August 2017 by Bitcoin developers who aimed to solve inefficiencies in Bitcoin. Typically, a block size in Bitcoin is limited to 1MB, with only seven transactions that can be verified per second. This pales in comparison to other digital transactions like Visa, which can process up to 56000 transactions per second.

BCH solved this problem by increasing the block size to 8MB, which means more transactions could be processed per second. This was achieved by removing the Segregated Witness protocol, which limits the block space in Bitcoin. As of February 2021, BCH had a market capitalization of $10.1 billion with about 18.67 billion BCH in circulation, each priced at $541.58. Its average daily turnover was $4.1 billion.

Stellar (XLM) - The Stellar network was launched in 2014 and is powered by Stellar Lumens token (XLM). It is an open blockchain aimed at facilitating large transactions between financial institutions. On average, it takes several days to transfer significantly large amounts between financial institutions, and the transaction would typically involve several intermediaries, making the cost of these transactions high. The Stellar network serves to ensure almost instantaneous settlement of these transactions with no intermediaries, lowering the transaction cost. It allows cross-border transaction of both fiat and cryptocurrencies. Using Stellar is free for both institutions and individuals.

Although it was designed for enterprise solutions, Stellar is an open blockchain and can thus be used by anyone. However, users must hold XML to transact on the network. As of February 2021, there were 22,522,341,144 XLM in circulation with a market capitalization of $9.6 billion. Each XLM cost $0.4262 and had a daily turnover of about $1.39 billion.

Dogecoin (DOGE) - Dogecoin was launched in December 2013 by Billy Markus and Jackson Palmer. It has a Scrypt Proof-of-Work consensus mechanism. Mining one block of Dogecoin creates 100000 new

DOGE. Although its developers created it to be a fun currency, the "meme culture" and its decent functionality propelled it to stardom.

Originally, the developers had set an upper limit of 100 billion DOGE but later altered the algorithm to allow for unlimited supply. As of February 2021, there was about 128.59 DOGE in circulation with a market capitalization of $6.58 billion. Each DOGE was $0.05099 with an average daily turnover of $1.57 billion.

Monero (XMR) - Monero was launched in 2014. It is of the most popular privacy coins. A privacy coin is a type of cryptocurrency that deliberately obfuscates a transactions link. This ensures that the wallet activity between the transacting parties remain anonymous and cannot be tracked. It becomes impossible to establish the transaction history or the funds that a particular wallet holds with cryptographic obscuring.

Monero uses 'Ring signatures' to cloak the sender's identity and the recipient of the crypto. When you initiate a transaction, a group of signers sign the transaction, which hides the actual sender's identity. Think of this as buying a gift for a colleague but having your entire office sign the card. This way, they won't know who bought the gift unless you tell them. In this case, if you send Monero to someone, they won't know you are the sender.

A Monero sender will generate a one-time 'spend key' that the recipient can only detect. The recipient is the only person who can spend the crypto using that key. Monero also uses stealth addresses which generates a one-time public key for recipients. It ensures that the fund being received is not directly connected to your wallet, but miners can verify that this transaction occurred, preventing the double-spending problem. More so, the Ring Confidential Transactions (RCT) masks the amount being sent and received. RCT is used as proof that Monero is not being used fraudulently. For example, if your wallet has 6 Monero and you only intend to send 2, you will have to send the whole balance of 5, then receive back 3.

As of February 2021, there were 17.85 million XMR in circulation with a market capitalization of $4.062 billion. XMR was priced at $227.55 and had an average daily turnover of about $630.4 million.

2.3 Key Milestones in The Crypto Industry

Since the launch of Bitcoin in 2008. The cryptocurrency market has undergone a series of milestones. Here are the most significant ones:

2008: the domain name Bitcoin.org is registered on August 18. Later, on October 31, Satoshi Nakamoto published the white paper: Bitcoin: A peer-to-peer Electronic Cash System. These two events led to the birth of cryptocurrency as we know it today.

2009: January 8, Bitcoin's code is made public. On January 12, the first-ever Bitcoin transaction was also recorded when Satoshi Nakamoto sent 10 BTC to Hal Finney. The first Bitcoin exchange rate was set in October 2009, where the US $1 was =1309.03 BTC.

2010: First commercial transaction involving BTC was recorded on May 22, when 10000 BTC was used to purchase pizza.

2011: Rival cryptocurrencies begin to emerge – they are called altcoins. This is precipitated by the popularity of decentralized and encrypted currencies. The first altcoin was Litecoin (LTC), which aimed to improve on inefficiencies inherent in BTC. It was launched on October 7, 2010. The first cryptocurrency exchanges – Bitstamp and Kraken – were formed in 2011. Crypto exchanges have played the most significant role in making cryptocurrencies mainstream.

2013: BTC reaches $1,000 for the first time, and its price crashes to below $300. It wasn't until 2015 when BTC hit $1,000 again. This was caused by the failure of holders to agree on new rules governing transactions, which resulted in the Bitcoin fork. For about six hours, there were two parallel networks. The first-ever Bitcoin ATM was launched in Vancouver in October 2013.

2014: The crypto exchange Mt. Gox went offline, resulting in a loss of 850,000 Bitcoins.

2015 – 2016: ICO craze started with Ethereum. The Ethereum platform made it the Rockstar of cryptocurrencies since it supports blockchain-based smart contracts and apps. It can be argued that most altcoins owe their existence to Ethereum. The ICO success of Ethereum marked the beginning of several other cryptos issuing ICOs driven by the public's appetite.

2017: Bitcoin fork occurs giving birth to Bitcoin Cash (BCH). Here, Bitcoin was split into two distinct cryptocurrencies – BTC and BCH. Japan also passed a law that recognized BTC as a legal payment method. In Norway, BTC is accepted as a payment system and an investment asset. BTC reaches $10,000 for the first time, driven by increasing popularity. Top global banks, including Barclays, Citi, and BNP Paribas, were mulling possible incorporation of BTC into their operations.

2018: European governments strategize on ways forward regarding the regulatory framework of cryptocurrencies. Samsung also confirmed that it would make chips designed to mine cryptocurrencies. This solidified the fact that cryptos are here to stay.

2019 – 2020: Ethereum launched ETH 2.0, which, among other things, is set to replace the Proof-of-Work with the Proof-of-Stake consensus mechanism. The staking concept introduced in ETH 2.0 enhances scalability and produces passive income for the stakers.

Institutional crypto investors surpassed retail traders. Thanks to the coronavirus pandemic, institutional and high net worth investors flocked to cryptocurrencies seeking a proper store of value for their wealth. This was a direct result of the inflation anticipated from the expansionary monetary and fiscal policies globally. In December 2020, the price of BTC crossed the $19,000 for the first time since December 2017. Closing the year at historic highs of $28,992.

In 2020, the US Office of the Comptroller of the Currency (OCC) authorized US banks to provide custodial services to cryptocurrency holders. On November 9, 2020, the US SEC also gave the nod to cryptocurrencies and digital assets.

Session 3
The Current Scenario

3.1 Everything About The 2021 Bull Market

2020 saw the longest and the most aggressive bull market for cryptocurrencies in history. In the first 60 days of 2021, cryptocurrencies have enjoyed an unprecedented bull market. Between January 2021 and March 2021, the entire crypto market's total market capitalization surged from $771.861 billion to $1.495 trillion.

However, to understand the crypto bull market of 2021, we must examine its origins from 2020. The total market capitalization of cryptocurrencies has increased from $188.273 billion in January 2020 to historic highs of $1.688 trillion in February 2021. Here are the most significant causes of this bull run:

Increased Demand

Remember that cryptocurrencies are inherently scarce. Nearly all the top cryptos have their maximum supply capped. Even for those with an unlimited supply, the rate at which more coins are added into circulation is slow and calculated. This means that we cannot expect millions of cryptos to be added to the market overnight. That is thanks to the slow crypto-mining process, which requires solving complex cryptographic equations. Since the supply of cryptocurrencies is finite, their price solely depends on demand. Going by the laws of supply and demand, if supply remains unchanged, and an increase in demand leads to increased prices. Conversely, when demand drops, the price will drop.

2020 saw the highest demand for cryptocurrencies since the launch of Bitcoin in 2008. This was primarily driven by the coronavirus pandemic and the aggressive expansionary monetary and fiscal policies that ensued. When COVID-19 ravaged global economies, governments globally implemented expansionary fiscal policies such as tax cuts and issuing stimulus cheques to their citizens. This was meant to stimulate expenditure in the economy and prevent an irreversible economic recession. Similarly, central banks adopted expansionary monetary policies by cutting interest rates to historic lows – some went into negative territories. This was also meant to encourage borrowing at low costs, stimulating expenditure within the economy. While these expansionary policies managed to prevent the worst-case scenario economically, they posed a significant threat to fiat currencies' value and stability.

The value of fiat currencies entirely depends on a country's economic performance, monetary and fiscal policies. Typically, when the economy performs well, the currency value increases. But a combination of expansionary fiscal and monetary policies threatened hyperinflation in the economy. Inflation is caused by a rapid increase in money supply coupled with a contracting economy. Consequently, the purchasing power of money rapidly decreases. That means that the value of the money you have now will be lower in future. This fear of inflation is what drove investors, both institutional and individual, to purchase cryptocurrencies. Remember that cryptocurrencies are decentralized — hence, any monetary and fiscal policies do not impact their value.

Naturally, the astronomical increase in demand led to the surge in the prices of cryptocurrencies. This bull run continued throughout 2020 and split over into 2021 as there are no signs of the end to the coronavirus. More so, the quantitative easing measures do not seem to have an end in sight, nor are governments pumping brakes on their domestic stimulus programs.

Bitcoin Halving

Throughout the 11-year history of cryptocurrencies, Bitcoin's market capitalization has consistently dominated the entire crypto market. It has always been above 60%. Due to its dominance, Bitcoin's bull run has a contagion impact on other cryptocurrencies. When the price of Bitcoin increases, altcoins also benefit. Bitcoin halving can best be described as an inbuilt anti-inflation mechanism within Bitcoin's code. Typically, Bitcoin miners are rewarded in BTC, which increases the supply of Bitcoins in circulation. Halving means that the miners' reward decreases by half after every 210000 blocks have been mined. This occurs approximately every four years. So, how does this affect the price of BTC?

We've already mentioned that the rate at which new Bitcoins are released into the market is on a distribution schedule and strictly based on a specific formula. Note that miners' rewards contribute to the increase in the supply of Bitcoin. Thus, when the reward is cut by half, it implies that the rate at which more Bitcoin is added into the market decreases — hence the term anti-inflationary mechanism.

Remember that Bitcoin has a finite supply. If you combined this with a decrease in the rate of increase in supply and increasing demand, then the price is bound to surge. Historically, Bitcoin has experienced a massive bull run once halving occurs. In the first Bitcoin halving in November 2012, Bitcoin experienced a bull run with its price spiking from $12 to $1150 in about 12 months. Another halving that occurred in 2016 led to a bull run that resulted in the price of BTC hitting $19000 by December 2017. The bull run of May 2020 resulted in a bull run with the price of BTC surging from just above $8000 to historic highs of $56799 in February 2021.
Consequently, Bitcoin's bull run spills over to altcoins. They benefit from it.

Fear of Missing Out (FOMO)

By design, the value of cryptos is entirely based on sentimental value. Over the years, the popularity of cryptocurrencies has been driven by increased demand due to the fear of missing out. People are driven to purchase cryptos because they see sensational media headlines regarding cryptos or others buying cryptos. Typically, most average crypto investors and traders are only in it because others are in it.

From 2020 to 2021, media headlines have been awash with positive crypto news. This has driven many retail and institutional traders to invest in cryptos. Subsequently, the increased demand fueled the bull run of 2020. In 2021, headlines about public companies investing in crypto triggered massive bull runs. For example, when Tesla Inc announced that it had invested $1.5 billion in BTC on February 8, 2021, the crypto gained about 14% in under two hours. The subsequent BTC bull run led to it attaining historic highs of $58354.14 on February 21, 2021.

The Explosion of Decentralized Finance (DeFi)

In the current age of rampant state surveillance, privacy is increasingly becoming a luxury that many cannot within the centralized financial system. DeFi offers every function from the traditional financial ecosystem on blockchain. Decentralized finance, at its core, is the provision of conventional financial services on platforms built on the public blockchain. Specifically, DeFi is based on the Ethereum blockchain platform. DeFi is heralded as the most suitable alternative to the global financial system. The biggest selling point for DeFi isn't just privacy; it solves all the centralized financial system's bottlenecks. These include creating open lending protocols and decentralized prediction markets, which effectively eliminated borders and nationality.

In 2020, there was a rise in the need for passive income, especially from crypto holders. As many people avoided trading cryptocurrencies to avoid volatility, DeFi provided the perfect platform for them to earn passive income from their crypto holdings. One of the greatest advancements made by DeFi is the creation of smart contracts. Smart contracts used in Ethereum refer to contracts that automatically execute when the terms agreed upon by the parties are attained. Unlike conventional contracts whose execution depends on counterparties and including a third party, the agreement terms in smart contracts are written within lines of codes. In this case, the contract executes itself, with the transaction being irreversible and transparent for all parties.

Note that, as is with anything on a blockchain network, the smart contract is decentralized. The most notable achievement of smart contracts is to enforce trust between anonymous parties eliminating the need for external enforcement mechanisms, legal systems, or central authority.

The demand for these products led to increased demand for cryptocurrencies, powering the bull run of 2020 into 2021.

Mainstream Acceptance of Cryptocurrencies

During the nascent years of cryptocurrencies, governments and financial institutions shunned them. They were not recognized as a means of payment but merely fringe assets. As the adoption and demand for cryptocurrencies and crypto assets increased over the years, financial regulators globally started paying attention. This came to a head in 2020, with most developed countries accepting cryptocurrencies as a means of payment and medium of exchange.

On July 22, 2020, the Office of the Comptroller of the Currency (OCC) directed national banks and federal savings associations' authority to provide cryptocurrency custody services. November 9, 2020, the US Securities and Exchange Commission (SEC) classified Bitcoin as tradable security while the Commodity Futures Trading Commission (CFTC) has categorized it as a commodity.

Note that regulation of cryptocurrencies and crypto assets do not compromise their decentralized nature. Regulations serve to protect the public from loss of money. One could argue that regulation has allowed institutions and public companies to add cryptocurrencies to the balance sheet. The consequent mainstream adoption of cryptocurrencies resulted in retail traders being displaced by institutional investors as most traders in cryptocurrencies. Some of the most notable companies investing in cryptocurrencies include Tesla, MicroStrategy Inc., and Square Inc., which are publicly traded companies. More so, global payment companies like PayPal and Visa also facilitate payment via crypto. This has increased the demand for cryptos for transactional purposes.

According to the US Futures Trading Commission, the adoption of the Proof-of-Stake model could change the classification of ETH from commodity to security. It means that US regulators, including the SEC, will acknowledge ETH as security. Furthermore, the CFTC chairman has voiced the optimism of regulators about DeFi. Their optimism primarily comes from the fact that they understand the burgeoning field of decentralized finance will not dissipate into oblivion. While the novel products introduced through DeFi pose a challenge, he believed that bringing them under the fold of rigorous scrutiny by financial regulators will ensure transparency and no price manipulation.

Growth of Crypto Derivatives

The growth of crypto derivatives in 2020 helped free up cryptos held in cold storages and spurred demand for crypto trading, which helped sustain the bull run. One of the most common arguments among critics of cryptocurrencies has been that the market is highly illiquid. This stems from the fact that crypto whales control a significant portion of cryptocurrencies stored in cold storages. It is estimated that merely 38% of all crypto are traded in the spot market.

Crypto derivatives serve to free up the held cryptos and bring liquidity back into the market. With derivatives, one doesn't need to own the underlying cryptocurrency. Derivatives drove up the need for investors to hedge against potential price volatility. In 2020, crypto derivatives grew to represent about 54% of the total transactions in the crypto market. they have played an important role in price discovery

Geopolitics

2020 has seen increased geopolitical events that have resulted in an erratic fluctuation in fiat currencies. These events include the uncertainty surrounding Brexit and trade wars between the EU, US and China. The geopolitical tensions have led to an increased demand for globally accepted currencies that are not bound by the geopolitical climate. Cryptocurrencies rose to fill this need. Stablecoins have emerged as best suited for transactional purposes. These coins have their value pegged on other assets.

They include crypto-collateralized coins, fiat-collateralized, and non-collateralized stable coins. For the non-collateralized stablecoins, algorithms are used to determine their value. Their value remains relatively stable and isn't susceptible to the volatility inherent in cryptocurrencies. Stable coins have helped increase demand in the crypto ecosystem.

Investors are switching to cryptocurrencies not just for speculative purposes but as a store of value as well.

Let's take an example of EUR/ETH and EUR/USD. In 2020, the USD weakened about 6.7% against the EUR, while ETH has strengthened about 306% against the EUR. From this perspective, it would have been better using the ETH both for speculative purposes and as a store of value would have been better.

3.2 Market Capitalization & Trading Volume of Major Cryptocurrencies

Market capitalization is the total market value of a cryptocurrency. It is calculated by multiplying the current price of the crypto by the total number of cryptos in circulation. i.e.,

Market capitalization = Price x number of coins in circulation

It is important to note that market capitalization is dynamic. It changes every second. That is because the supply of cryptocurrencies is constantly increasing in the market due to the mining process. Even for cryptos whose supply is fixed, the constant fluctuation in price guarantees that the market capitalization of cryptocurrencies never remains the same.

The list includes cryptocurrencies with a market capitalization of above $1 billion as of **March 2021.**

Note - The * sign implies that those cryptos cannot be mined.

#	Name	Symbol	Market Cap	Price	Circulating Supply
1	Bitcoin	BTC	$ 876,378,302,015	$47,003.70	18,644,881 BTC
2	Ethereum	ETH	$171,617,722,268	$1,493.40	114,917,419 ETH
3	Tether	USDT	$36,376,534,238	$1.00	36,364,902,054 USDT *
4	Binance Coin	BNB	$34,206,488,520	$221.35	154,532,785 BNB *
5	Cardano	ADA	$34,152,846,014	$1.07	31,948,309,441 ADA
6	Polkadot	DOT	$31,144,853,427	$34.03	915,164,829 DOT *

7	XRP	XRP	$21,060,93 2,060	$0.46	45,404,02 8,640 XRP *
8	Uniswap	UNI	$11,721,45 0,344	$26.93	435,269,9 13 UNI *
9	Litecoin	LTC	$11,575,47 8,909	$173.8 2	66,595,48 8 LTC
1 0	Chainlink	LINK	$11,002,16 6,128	$26.83	410,009,5 56 LINK *
1 1	Bitcoin Cash	BCH	$9,165,349 ,876	$490.8 9	18,670,92 5 BCH
1 2	Stellar	XLM	$9,021,727 ,515	$0.40	22,571,07 0,085 XLM *
1 3	USD Coin	USD C	$8,657,440 ,546	$1.00	8,654,680, 801 USDC *

1 4 Dogecoin	DO GE	$6,235,845 ,783	$0.05	128,619,3 70,524 DOGE
1 5 NEM	XEM	$6,005,813 ,237	$0.67	8,999,999, 999 XEM *
1 6 Wrapped BTC	WBT C	$5,812,808 ,399	$46,96 4.57	123,770 WBTC *
1 7 Aave	AAV E	$4,490,736 ,587	$361.4 4	12,424,46 8 AAVE *
1 8 THETA	THET A	$4,248,042 ,849	$4.25	1,000,000, 000 THETA *
1 9 Cosmos	ATO M	$3,862,450 ,732	$18.28	211,305,5 91 ATOM *
2 0 Monero	XMR	$3,764,814 ,296	$210.8 6	17,854,58 0 XMR

2 1	TRON	TRX	$3,560,555 ,801	$0.05	71,659,65 7,369 TRX *
2 2	Crypto.c om	CRO	$3,547,782 ,649	$0.15	24,143,83 5,615 CRO *
2 3	EOS	EOS	$3,477,764 ,768	$3.66	951,054,0 64 EOS *
2 4	IOTA	MIO TA	$3,365,940 ,559	$1.21	2,779,530, 283 MIÓTA *
2 5	Solana	SOL	$3,335,775 ,911	$12.74	261,900,1 37 SOL *
2 6	Bitcoin SV	BSV	$3,320,000 ,023	$177.8 4	18,668,92 7 BSV
2 7	VeChain	VET	$3,073,590 ,196	$0.05	64,315,57

					6,989 VET *
2 8	Terra	LUN A	$2,955,471 ,505	$7.23	408,504,2 98 LUNA *
2 9	Binance USD	BUS D	$2,922,554 ,226	$1.00	2,922,846, 511 BUSD *
3 0	Huobi Token	HT	$2,820,040 ,076	$15.09	186,866,5 18 HT *
3 1	FTX Token	FTT	$2,697,945 ,576	$28.60	94,346,95 8 FTT *
3 2	Tezos	XTZ	$2,695,535 ,071	$3.54	762,047,9 09 XTZ *
3 3	Neo	NEO	$2,583,240 ,189	$36.62	70,538,83 1 NEO *

3 4	Dai	DAI	$2,547,484,234	$1.00	2,544,683,868 DAI *
3 5	Elrond	EGL D	$2,445,164,057	$143.30	17,063,226 EGLD *
3 6	Syntheti x	SNX	$2,389,220,314	$20.80	114,841,533 SNX *
3 7	Algoran d	ALG O	$2,301,245,770	$1.04	2,215,140,145 ALGO *
3 8	Filecoin	FIL	$2,269,940,300	$39.54	57,415,312 FIL
3 9	The Graph	GRT	$2,237,713,224	$1.80	1,245,666,867 GRT *
4 0	Compou nd	CO MP	$2,121,267,470	$456.08	4,651,041 COMP *

4 1	SushiSwap	SUSHI	$2,117,184,363	$16.64	127,244,443 SUSHI *
4 2	Maker	MKR	$2,087,432,679	$2,097.42	995,239 MKR *
4 3	Dash	DASH	$2,042,944,490	$204.13	10,008,171 DASH
4 4	Kusama	KSM	$1,882,472,621	$222.25	8,470,098 KSM *
4 5	UNUS LEO	LEO	$1,876,582,869	$1.88	999,498,893 LEO *
4 6	Avalanche	AVAX	$1,853,834,340	$24.10	76,937,055 AVAX *
4 7	Decred	DCR	$1,760,341,450	$138.93	12,670,606 DCR

4 8	Pancake Swap	CAK E	$1,395,168 ,340	$11.09	125,775,2 96 CAKE *
4 9	Zcash	ZEC	$1,330,090 ,510	$118.1 0	11,262,43 1 ZEC
5 0	NEAR Protocol	NEA R	$1,305,766 ,553	$4.25	307,336,8 84 NEAR *
5 1	Zilliqa	ZIL	$1,261,858 ,911	$0.11	11,015,43 9,934 ZIL
5 2	Ethereu m Classic	ETC	$1,246,680 ,942	$10.72	116,313,2 99 ETC
5 3	Voyager Token	VGX	$1,223,215 ,201	$5.50	222,295,2 08 VGX *
5 4	THORCh ain	RUN E	$1,204,761 ,739	$5.06	238,275,7 61 RUNE *

5 5	Nexo	NEX O	$1,201,707 ,041	$2.15	560,000,0 11 NEXO *
5 6	Bitcoin BEP2	BTC B	$1,197,590 ,889	$47,34 3.55	25,296 BTCB *
5 7	Ravencoi n	RVN	$1,174,482 ,233	$0.14	8,263,870, 000 RVN
5 8	BitTorren t	BTT	$1,160,696 ,531	$0.00	989,947,8 25,856 BTT *
5 9	Yearn.fi nance	YFI	$1,143,663 ,254	$31,21 7.83	36,635 YFI *
6 0	Hedera Hashgra ph	HBA R	$1,139,099 ,108	$0.15	7,514,692, 399 HBAR *
6 1	UMA	UMA	$1,125,827 ,943	$20.04	56,166,65 3 UMA *

6 2	Fantom	FTM	$1,092,412 ,926	$0.43	2,545,006, 273 FTM *
6 3	ICON	ICX	$1,085,346 ,695	$1.83	592,080,1 59 ICX *
6 4	Celsius	CEL	$1,061,972 ,235	$4.45	238,863,5 20 CEL *
6 5	Revain	REV	$1,047,486 ,780	$0.01	85,061,48 5,690 REV *
6 6	Enjin Coin	ENJ	$1,044,065 ,260	$1.25	834,313,7 57 ENJ *
6 7	0x	ZRX	$1,002,713 ,983	$1.32	760,407,2 32 ZRX *

Trading Volume

The trading volume is the total value of a cryptocurrency that has been traded within the previous 24 hours. This is an important metric because it helps us determine the popularity of crypto. It represents the trading activity surrounding particular crypto, which can be essential when planning your trading and investment activities. However, note that the trading volume we've calculated here is based on publicly available data. Significant trade volumes may occur privately in OTC markets.

The most important use of crypto trading volume is to identify healthy cryptocurrencies. Theoretically, crypto may appear sound, but if it doesn't have trades, then it poses a significant threat to your portfolio. This could indicate that the crypto is held by a few whales who might manipulate prices to their advantage. More so, since trading involves buying and selling, it helps make the process of crypto price discovery more efficient. Thus, the higher the trading volume, the more efficient and fairer the crypto price is.

Traders can also use trading volume to identify opportunities to buy or short crypto. Here's an example. Say you are monitoring a particular crypto, and you notice that the trading volume is steadily increasing. This could be a sign to go long since, for cryptos, an increase in demand corresponds with a price increase. Conversely, if you notice that the trading volume of a particular crypto is dropping drastically, it could indicate that its demand is waning. This often precedes a drop in the price. Typically, when the trading volume decreases, it implies that investors are pessimistic about particular crypto. It is an indicator that they are taking profits, and there is no sufficient demand to absorb the selling.

In the crypto market, trading volume often corresponds with price volatility. Cryptocurrencies with higher trading volumes tend to have relatively stables and less volatile prices. For the market price significantly, a large number of buyers and sellers are needed. This makes trading cryptos with higher trading volume safer, but there is less room for profitability since volatility sometimes comes with increased profitability. Note that if crypto has an abnormal trading volume, it could indicate that it is trading at inflated prices. This is especially true when there are sudden spikes in trading volume.

Here's a list of the trading volume of the major cryptocurrencies.

Rank	Name	Symbol	24-Hour Trading Volume
3	Tether	USDT	$102,249,530,264
1	Bitcoin	BTC	$51,524,550,665
2	Ethereum	ETH	$22,600,073,744
5	Cardano	ADA	$7,281,874,864
7	XRP	XRP	$6,024,423,346
4	Binance Coin	BNB	$5,526,324,851
9	Litecoin	LTC	$5,435,425,926
29	Binance USD	BUSD	$3,909,417,414
11	Bitcoin Cash	BCH	$3,673,610,902
21	TRON	TRX	$2,902,876,655

6	Polkadot	DOT	$2,761,304,195
30	Huobi Token	HT	$2,614,158,727
23	EOS	EOS	$2,507,078,414
10	Chainlink	LINK	$1,912,137,331
66	Enjin Coin	ENJ	$1,825,913,031
8	Uniswap	UNI	$1,802,744,988
13	USD Coin	USDC	$1,625,685,354
14	Dogecoin	DOGE	$1,182,885,057
12	Stellar	XLM	$1,160,582,251
38	Filecoin	FIL	$1,073,994,796
52	Ethereum Classic	ETC	$1,035,364,072
43	Dash	DASH	$995,768,590

33	Neo	NEO	$779,273,213
19	Cosmos	ATOM	$756,581,054
15	NEM	XEM	$716,553,585
41	SushiSwap	SUSHI	$697,472,750
20	Monero	XMR	$696,722,683
26	Bitcoin SV	BSV	$680,833,123
27	VeChain	VET	$665,718,075
60	Hedera Hashgraph	HBAR	$552,329,010
37	Algorand	ALGO	$543,722,335
32	Tezos	XTZ	$500,079,251
49	Zcash	ZEC	$479,487,995
63	ICON	ICX	$461,538,762

18	THETA	THETA	$437,121,610
28	Terra	LUNA	$413,130,812
17	Aave	AAVE	$382,936,271
48	PancakeSwap	CAKE	$340,674,398
34	Dai	DAI	$340,265,731
35	Elrond	EGLD	$335,087,066
39	The Graph	GRT	$304,491,321
46	Avalanche	AVAX	$264,520,598
40	Compound	COMP	$249,358,813
62	Fantom	FTM	$231,039,754
58	BitTorrent	BTT	$224,562,859
59	yearn.finance	YFI	$221,579,440

22	Crypto.com Coin	CRO	$221,414,008
24	IOTA	MIOTA	$215,605,435
36	Synthetix	SNX	$183,642,984
67	0x	ZRX	$183,543,489
51	Zilliqa	ZIL	$178,111,576
44	Kusama	KSM	$171,020,182
16	Wrapped Bitcoin	WBTC	$160,237,527
57	Ravencoin	RVN	$135,165,722
25	Solana	SOL	$115,287,255
50	NEAR Protocol	NEAR	$115,002,751
31	FTX Token	FTT	$99,533,079

42	Maker	MKR	$94,533,708
54	THORChain	RUNE	$58,218,768
61	UMA	UMA	$40,025,037
56	Bitcoin BEP2	BTCB	$30,696,771
47	Decred	DCR	$23,050,980
53	Voyager Token	VGX	$18,054,497
55	Nexo	NEXO	$7,922,374
64	Celsius	CEL	$5,171,260
65	Revain	REV	$3,497,961
45	UNUS SED LEO	LEO	$656,374

3.3 Price Analysis of Bitcoin and Top Altcoins

The correlation between BTC and top altcoins' price is undeniable for any seasoned crypto investors or trader. The cryptocurrency market is closely knit, and often, the price of altcoins tends to correlate with that of BTC highly.

The primary reason behind this is that Bitcoin has enjoyed market dominance among cryptocurrencies for the longest time. Although there are over 5000 cryptocurrencies in circulation, as of March 2021, BTC market capitalization accounted for 68.1% of the entire crypto market. Since there is no fundamental algorithm to determine the price of altcoins, their prices follow BTC's price, which is seen as the "gold standard" in the crypto ecosystem.

The price discovery occurs with trading. Thus, an increase in demand for Bitcoin on crypto exchanges is positive for altcoins. That's because a bull run follows the increased demand for BTC followed by a contagion throughout the market.

Take a look at the chart below. We've compared the trend in the price of top altcoins with Bitcoin from January till March 2021. The correlation pattern is easily noticeable. The fluctuation in the prices of altcoins mimics that of BTC.

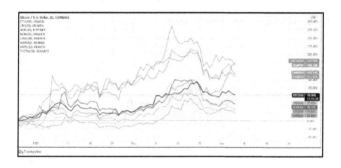

The cryptocurrency market follows the principle of "first mover's advantage". Since Bitcoin is the original crypto, the value of altcoins tends to be based around it. We mentioned earlier that the value of cryptos almost entirely depends on their demand. Therefore, the value in the entire crypto market is solely subjective.

However, the positive correlation between BTC and top altcoins doesn't always hold. This can be explained by the emergence and subsequent popularity of DeFi, whose platform is built on Ethereum. This means that BTC isn't compatible with DeFi, and users must convert their BTC to other altcoins which are compatible with the DeFi platform. Naturally, this lowers the demand for BTC and consequently a drop in its price, while the demand and altcoins price increase.

3.4 Credible Sources to Find Information on Cryptos

As cryptocurrencies exploded into mainstream finance over the years, several platforms and crypto products are developing faster than ever. Currently, there are over 5000 cryptocurrencies with new crypto-related products rolled out almost every day, which makes it difficult, even for a seasoned crypto investor, to keep up. Naturally, there are countless phony experts for a growing industry like crypto.

Note: We also highly recommend that you visit the official websites of specific cryptos. You can also check the verified social media accounts of top crypto executives.

Credible information is hard to come by. This makes doing your own research valuable. Here are the most competent and trustworthy sources of information regarding cryptocurrencies:

CoinMarketCap - As the name suggests, CoinMarketCap tracks the up-to-the-minute valuation of all known cryptocurrencies. This includes their price, market capitalization, and 24-hour traded volume. It also ranks cryptocurrency spot exchanges, derivative exchanges, decentralized exchanges, and lending exchanges.

CoinDesk - CoinDesk is the most reliable and one of the oldest new websites. It provides news updates, educational articles, and market trends. It was established in 2013.

CoinTelegraph - CoinTelegraph provides short, easy-to-read articles about cryptocurrencies and crypto products.

Blockonomi - Started in 2017, Blockonomi provides informational, analysis and educational content relating to the crypto market.

Bitcoin.com - Bitcoin.com provides up-to-date news and analysis on the cryptocurrency market.

Reddit - Reddit has one of the largest crypto community for investors and traders. Here, you can communicate with members and ask any questions for which you'll receive multiple feedbacks. This is one of the best ways to expand your knowledge of cryptocurrencies. You can sign up for the <u>liquid subreddit</u> here.

Session 4
Cryptocurrency Trading vs. Investing

4.1 The Difference Between Trading and Investing

The burgeoning cryptocurrency market has attracted various types of participant. The most dominant ones are crypto traders and investors. Although both trading and investing have the same end goal – making money, there are several fundamental differences between them.

Trading involves buying or selling cryptocurrencies over the short term – i.e., going long or short. Trading focusses on maximizing short-term gains by taking advantage of volatility and media hype. Traders often spend most of their time observing chart patterns and analyzing trends before deciding whether to go short or long.

Most traders also use proprietary tools and techniques to enhance their profits. They also take advantage of the various order types to help them open and close positions under specific market conditions. Risk management techniques such as the use of leverage and stop-loss levels are also handy to traders.

In a nutshell, traders aim to profit in the market by taking advantage of short-term volatility. Primarily, most traders use leverage to increase the size of their positions and magnify their potential profits. More so, traders often prefer to trade contract for difference (CFD) assets than own the underlying assets.

Investing: involves buying and holding an asset over the longer term. Investing is focused on the bigger picture, and investors tend to ignore the shorter-term price fluctuation and concentrate on the fundamental quality of the asset.

The primary goal of investors is to attain the maximum possible return on investment by holding as an asset for the maximum duration possible. In investing, it is believed that in the long run, the asset will appreciate; that is why investors will overlook the short-term price volatility and even continue accumulating their portfolio size when the price is low.

Note that investing involves buying and owning the actual asset. For example, a Bitcoin investor will buy and receive BTC in their wallet. This means that there is no leverage involved when investing. One of the most significant advantages of investing is that if the market crashes, you will only lose the equivalent of the amount you have invested. However, this is rarely the case since it is unheard of for the price of an asset to drop to $0. Compared to trading, a small market shift in the opposite direction could wipe out a trader's capital and sometimes run a negative balance when using leverage.

Here's a table showing the fundamental differences between trading and investing.

Trading	Investing
Traders are focused on short-term gains	Investors focus on longer-term profitability
Trading involves the use of leverage	No leverage is involved in investing

Most traders prefer CFDs	One owns the underlying asset when investing
Technical analysis is the most preferred method by traders	Investors focus on the fundamental analysis
Traders can go long or short depending on price fluctuation	Investing involves buying and holding an asset

4.2 Introduction to Crypto Exchanges & Wallets

What is a Crypto Exchange?

Crypto exchanges have played a significant role in popularizing cryptocurrencies. They've achieved this by making the process of price discovery more efficient and increasing transparency in crypto trading. It is thanks to crypto exchanges that crypto derivatives surpassed spot trading. As of March 2021, crypto derivatives account for about 56% of all transactions in the crypto market.

The simplest definition of s cryptocurrency exchange is an online platform where users can buy cryptocurrencies using fiat currencies or exchange one crypto for another. Most of the crypto exchanges also perform leveraged crypto trading by allowing users to bet on price movement. Apart from trading in the spot market, several futures contracts are also available for trading on crypto exchanges.

Types of Crypto Exchanges

1. Centralized Crypto Exchanges (CEX)

These are the traditional type of crypto exchanges that are modelled after centralized stock exchanges. This means that the exchange is a third party responsible for ensuring that transactions between buyers and sellers go smoothly. Since the exchange matches buyers and sellers, it charges a transaction fee for every transaction. Some CEXs impose minimum and maximum transaction limits.

CEXs often comply with strict Know Your Customer (KYC) and Anti-Money Laundering (AML) regulations. That means if you expect absolute privacy, such exchanges are not ideal for you. Coinbase and Kraken are examples of centralized crypto exchanges.

2. Decentralized Crypto Exchange (DEX)

These are online crypto exchanges based on blockchain technology. It means that no single entity controls the exchange since it is autonomous and independent. There are no KYC or AML policies required when using the DEXs. These exchanges only serve to route and match the purchase and sale orders in the network. AirSwap, EtherDelta, and WavesDex are examples of decentralized exchanges.

3. Peer-to-Peer (P2P) Crypto Exchanges

These exchanges are also called direct crypto exchanges because they are designed to facilitate crypto exchange between individuals. In such crypto exchanges, there is no consensus market price for particular crypto. Rather, buyers and sellers quote their preferred price and find suitable matches which can and willing to transact with them. Users are free to negotiate among themselves for the best possible terms. After an agreement of the terms of the transaction, both parties coordinate the transfer of cryptos and are free to select the mode of payment. In many instances, the direct crypto exchange also serves as escrow for the cryptocurrencies, which are then released to the buyer once payment has been received. Such crypto exchanges have proven to be vital in underdeveloped countries. However, before you engage in buying and selling on a P2P crypto exchange, ensure that you have checked the market price of the crypto you intend to purchase.

4. Crypto Brokers

Cryptocurrency brokers are similar to centralized crypto exchanges. However, crypto brokers set the prices at which a user can buy. Typically, this is often the market price plus a premium that enables the broker to profit. This model is similar to exchanging forex at your local bank. Note that transactions in this type of crypto exchange exclusively occur between the crypto broker and the user. There are no transactions between buyers and sellers. Crypto brokers are often the preferred platforms for individuals new to the crypto universe.

5. Cryptocurrency Funds

Crypto funds are professionally managed funds that allow users to purchase and invest in cryptocurrencies through the funds. Apart from offering professionally managed and diverse crypto portfolios, crypto funds help a user avoid the hassle of purchasing and storing cryptocurrencies. However, crypto funds are purely for investment purposes since one cannot use them for transactional purposes.

Crypto exchanges can also be categorized based on their functionalities. They can be; spot crypto exchanges, derivatives crypto exchanges, or lending crypto exchanges.

Importance of Crypto Exchanges

1. Allows hedging against volatility

Volatility is an inherent property of cryptocurrencies. One of the strongest arguments used by crypto critics is that cryptocurrencies are too unstable to be used as a medium of exchange. Crypto exchanges have stepped in to fill this with the introduction of crypto derivatives. Crypto derivatives allow merchants to accept cryptos as payment. They can then purchase futures derivatives and options that help protect the transactions they make in the spot market. This effectively removes the problem of volatility.

2. Freeing up liquidity

It is estimated that crypto whales hold over 45% of all cryptocurrencies in cold storages. This robs the crypto market of valuable liquidity. The growth and maturity of crypto exchanges created crypto derivatives that have facilitated the unlocking of the dormant cryptos to be used in lending and borrowing. Crypto derivatives include crypto CFDs, crypto futures and options, and crypto funds and ETFs. As of March 2021, crypto derivatives accounted for about 54% of all crypto transactions.

3. Ensures efficient crypto price discovery

There are three primary ways in which crypto exchanges have facilitated efficient crypto price discovery. Firstly, efficient price discovery has been achieved by freeing up liquidity in the market. With higher liquidity, price volatility is tamed since demand and supply are matched. For tradable assets, volatility tends to arise when there is a gross mismatch in demand and supply.

Secondly, crypto exchanges led to the growth of crypto derivatives. Crypto derivatives allowed traders to freely go long or short, unlike in the spot market where crypto investors dominate HODLing hence skewing the price. More so, these investors could easily manipulate the market prices to their advantage.

Thirdly, crypto exchanges help to match the buyers and sellers in real-time. This ensures there is no artificial accumulation of buy or sell orders which might skew the price of a crypto asset. By order matching, crypto exchanges not only ensure efficient price based on laws of supply and demand; they also foster pricing transparency in the crypto market.

4. Crypto Exchanges encourage faster adoption of cryptos

During the developing ages of cryptocurrencies, many would-be crypto investors and traders couldn't access crypto markets due to scarcity of information and pricing data. Crypto exchanges have increased the adoption of cryptocurrencies since they are trustworthy due to regulations. More so, crypto exchanges have made it easier for traders and investors to instantly buy and sell their portfolios by matching counterparties and eliminating counterparty risks. They have effectively guaranteed a near-instantaneous entry and exit, which brings convenience in trading and investing. This encourages adoption.

There are over 5000 cryptocurrencies in the market. Crypto exchanges have made it possible for traders and investors to easily access all these cryptos' pricing and market capitalization data. The quick access and availability of this information encourage diversification of portfolios.

What is a Crypto Wallet?

When you buy cryptocurrencies, you store them in a crypto wallet. A cryptocurrency wallet is a program that allows you to receive, send, and store cryptocurrencies. There are several types of cryptocurrency wallets. Some of them include desktop, mobile, online, hardware, and paper crypto wallets.

How do Crypto Wallets Work?

Technically, the cryptos aren't exactly stored in the wallet. They are stored on the coin's blockchain. Here's how it works. The public key keeps all the records of all transactions, and that's how it maintains your crypto balance. For example, if you have a BTC wallet, the wallet doesn't have BTC since BTC is on Bitcoin's blockchain. The crypto wallet is designed to interact with the blockchain. It stores crypto addresses and allows cryptos to be transferred between these addresses.

Cryptocurrency wallets have private and public keys.

Public key: is a long alphanumeric sequence which is your wallet's address. This is the address that people use to send cryptocurrencies to you. Think of it as your bank account number, which you can give to anyone to send or deposit money into your account.

Private key: is what you use to access the Cryptocurrency stored in your wallet. It is like the PIN to your bank account, which you should keep secret.

Note that not all wallets give you sole control of your private keys, which means you do not explicitly control the cryptos in your wallet. You shouldn't share your private key with anyone — they could easily access and transfer your cryptos.

Most crypto wallets are custodial wallets. With such wallets, all you have to worry about is the balance in your crypto wallet and your public address. You do not get the private key with a custodial wallet. On the other hand, full wallets have both private and public keys, both of which are connected to a public address. With custodial wallets, you do not have complete control of your private keys. Most crypto exchanges are custodial wallets. This means that they can move your funds without asking for explicit consent.

How to use a crypto wallet?

Crypto wallets have three primary functions — send, receive, and store cryptocurrencies.

Sending from a crypto wallet

Regardless of the type of crypto wallet you use, the procedure for sending cryptos is fairly standard.

However, for hardware crypto wallets, you must ensure that you are connected to the internet.

1. Long into your crypto wallet
2. Select the option of sending
3. Select the address of the recipient. Always remember that addresses are crypto-specific. That means if you are sending BTC, you must enter the recipient's BTC public address. If you send BTC to an ETH address, your crypto will be lost permanently since crypto transactions are irreversible.
4. Specify the amount you are sending. Check the applicable transaction fee to ensure you have sufficient crypto
5. Double-check all the details, enter your private key and then click 'send.'

Receiving cryptos to your crypto wallet
Although receiving cryptocurrencies is fairly easy, the process might vary depending on the crypto wallet. Some crypto wallets issue one public address, while others provide you with a public address for every transaction.

1. Log into your crypto wallet

2. Click 'Receive'

3. Copy the public address issued

4. Send the public address to whoever is sending you the funds

5. Wait for the funds to reflect in your wallet

Storing cryptos in your wallet

Once you've received cryptos in your wallet, you don't need to do much. You may log in now and then to confirm your crypto balance. Some crypto wallets also allow you to stake your cryptos and earn interest. The instructions for this are specific to the respective wallets.

Types of Crypto Wallets

Online crypto wallet: These crypto wallets are software stored in the cloud, meaning that you can access your software anywhere any time, provided you have an internet connection. You do not need to downline an app. However, since online crypto wallets are hosted by third parties, it increases the chances of your funds being stolen if the host suffers a malicious attack. The majority of crypto theft often happens when online crypto wallets are compromised.

Mobile crypto wallet: This is a crypto wallet in the form of an app run from your smartphone. While it provides a convenient mode to access your crypto, it is not entirely the safest crypto wallet.

Desktop crypto wallet: This is a crypto wallet in the form of an app you download and install on your PC. This crypto wallet can only be accessed from that particular computer, meaning if you lose your PC or a virus corrupts it, you will lose your cryptos. Always remember to create a backup.

Hardware crypto wallet: These wallets come in the form of hardware such as an external computer drive or a USB stick. Such wallets can specifically be designed to hold particular crypto or specific multiple cryptos. To access the cryptos stored in the hardware wallet, you'll have to connect to the internet wirelessly or plugin. Hardware crypto wallets are considered the safest since your cryptos are stored online and cannot be hacked. The only risk you face is if you lose or irreparably damage the wallet.

Paper crypto wallet: This wallet involves getting a QR code printout of both your public and private keys. It allows you to avoid storing any data digitally and be able to send and receive cryptos. Just make sure not to lose that paper!

How to choose a cryptocurrency wallet?

Here are some of the factors you should consider before choosing a crypto wallet

Ease of use: For beginners, sending and receiving cryptocurrencies can be tedious and complicated. Experienced traders and investors would prefer that the process of sending and receiving cryptos be as quick as possible, have advanced features and support as many cryptos as possible. Thus, selecting a crypto wallet should match your needs and experience. Beginner users can choose crypto wallets that are simple to set up and easy to access. Experienced users might prefer a crypto wallet that serves as an exchange and supports multi-signature transactions.

The type of wallet: The type of wallet you prefer. This could depend on the security features you prefer to have. If security is your utmost priority, then having hardware or paper wallets should be your preference. However, if you need the convenience of accessing your wallet on the go, mobile and online crypto wallets are preferable.

You should also consider crypto wallets with extra security features such as two-factor authentication and multi-sign functionality, whether you'll have complete access to your private keys, and if that crypto wallet has had incidences of a breach.

Cost: Typically, most online crypto wallets are free. However, if you need extra security and choose hardware wallets, you should consider the cost. Make sure to read the fine print since some wallets also charge a fee per transaction.

Supported cryptos: You should consider if you're looking for a crypto wallet that supports only single crypto or multiple cryptos. Ensure that the wallet you select is compatible with the cryptos you have. Also, note that some cryptos can only be stored in official wallets.

Holding Cryptos on an exchange vs in a wallet

Most beginners would prefer holding their cryptos in the wallets attached to the crypto exchange where they bought the cryptos. This is a convenient method, and you get to avoid the hassle of setting up or buying a crypto wallet. More so, you can access your cryptos any time. Although this is convenient, it is not encouraged because the crypto exchange controls your portfolio since you do not get a private key. This means that you do not fully own your cryptos. More so, crypto exchanges are the number one target for hackers. The most prominent crypto thefts in history are those of crypto exchanges.

How to keep your crypto wallet safe?

For any crypto owner, the security of their wallet is paramount. Here are some tips to keep your crypto wallet as safe as possible.

Research and compare the best crypto wallets. There is plenty of information online about every crypto wallet. Compare them and see if there are any security breach incidents and what user reviews say about a particular crypto wallet.

Enable two-factor authentication: It provides an extra layer of security for your wallet and makes it almost impossible for anyone to access your wallet without authorization

Choose a multi-signature wallet: A multi signature wallet requires more than one private to process a transaction. This means that two users with distinct private keys must sign in for a transaction to be authorized. Although this increases the time to process a single transaction, it is a small price to pay for well-deserved security.

Ensure you have a backup: Always create a backup of your crypto wallet so that you can recover your funds if your wallet is damaged or lost.

Never share your private key: Firstly, check if your crypto wallet allows you to keep your private keys. If it does, ensure it remains private.

4.3 Getting Started with Crypto Investing

Crypto investing involves buying cryptocurrencies to sell them when their price is higher. Naturally, when it comes to investing, investors often hold their cryptocurrencies over a longer time, ignoring short-term fluctuations. During the hold period, crypto investors often increase their crypto holding by accumulating more cryptos from the open market.

The primary goal of investors is to attain the maximum possible return on investment by holding as an asset for the maximum duration possible. In investing, it is believed that in the long run, the asset will appreciate; that is why investors will overlook the short-term price volatility and even continue accumulating their portfolio size when the price is low.

Note that investing involves buying and owning the actual asset. For example, a Bitcoin investor will buy and receive BTC in their wallet. This means that there is no leverage involved when investing. One of the most significant advantages of investing is that if the market crashes, you will only lose the equivalent of the amount you have invested. However, this is rarely the case since it is unheard of for the price of an asset to drop to $0. Compared to trading, a small market shift in the opposite direction could wipe out a trader's capital and sometimes run a negative balance when using leverage.

Why Invest in Cryptos?

Here's the main idea most crypto investors have in mind. Cryptocurrencies are immune to inflation since they are limited in supply. Unlike fiat currency, their value depends on demand. As cryptos are increasingly accepted in mainstream finance, their demand will increase exponentially, making them more valuable with time.

Decentralized finance is the future

The blockchain technology upon which cryptocurrencies are built has unlimited applications outside cryptocurrencies. The uses of this technology span every industry. From finance, healthcare, education, transport, democratic voting to the development of the new internet. The applications are limitless. As blockchain become increasingly adopted, more cryptocurrencies will be demanded transactions. And the more the demand, the higher the value.

Here's the catch, we cannot expect that every aspect of life becomes overhauled overnight and adaptable to the blockchain. This is where long term investing comes to play. Take, for example, when Bitcoin was rolled out back in 2008. There was skepticism that cryptocurrencies were a scam and that cryptocurrencies would have no real use. Since it started trading in August 2011, BTC has appreciated more than 498,000%!

Since Bitcoin, over 5000 cryptocurrencies have been developed, and over the past three years, their values have increased astronomically. This is thanks to decentralized finance (DeFi), which has expanded the applications and usability of cryptocurrencies. Arguably, DeFi is the future of finance.

A cryptocurrency investor should have a thick skin and have the mental fortitude to withstand a short-term market flash crash. Whether you are investing in cryptocurrencies or simply holding them as a store of value, you must have your sights trained for the long-haul. Remember that speculative crypto traders will always cause market volatility in the short-term, which will lead to price dips. That's because crypto traders can go long or short as they please. Bear crypto markets can also result from negative publicity such as crypto hacks that leads to loss of cryptos.

In the case of Bitcoin, if you plot the curve over the past decade, you'll notice the market slump between 2018 and 2019. This occurred after BTC hit highs of $19,666 in December 2017. During this period, the slump was fueled by the negative publicity that the price was inflated and was in a bubble since BTC is merely a virtual token that offers no real value. This prompted massive sell-off from crypto sceptics and earlier investors who embarked on profit-taking. Naturally, the price continued to drop.

Store of Value

It wasn't until 2020, at the onset of the coronavirus pandemic, that the true value of cryptocurrencies manifested in practical terms. The aggressive fiscal and monetary policies adopted globally by governments and central banks threatened the fiat monetary system with unprecedented inflation. Consequently, institutions and high net worth individuals migrated to cryptocurrencies to protect their investments.

As we've mentioned, cryptocurrencies are immune to such policies since they are decentralized and limited in supply. That makes them the ideal assets for a store of value and protecting purchasing power. For fiat currencies, a rise in inflation reduces their purchasing power, and monetary holdings lose value.

Publicly traded companies like MicroStrategy Inc. and Tesla amended their treasury reserve policies to adopt BTC as a reserve asset. These are among a legion of companies that invested billions of dollars in Bitcoin and planned to accept crypto as payment for goods and services. JP Morgan Chase estimates that more institutions will adopt cryptocurrencies.

Increased Mainstream Adoption

In the past, centralized finance vilified cryptocurrencies. Most financial institutions went as far as banning transactions involving cryptocurrencies, and several jurisdictions declared cryptocurrencies illegal. Over the years, their footing has shifted. Global banks are at the forefront of setting up crypto asset management units while financial services providers are developing payment systems dedicated to handling crypto transactions.

Mastercard announced on February 10 that it would start supporting cryptocurrencies on its network. Visa is developing an API system that would allow its client banks to facilitate crypto transactions seamlessly. PayPal rolled out a facility to support trading and hold of cryptos on its platform.

How to Invest in Cryptocurrencies?

Allocate a percentage of your wealth to cryptos

Keep in mind that investing in cryptocurrencies is a long-term strategy. Thus, you shouldn't allocate all your wealth to investing in cryptos. Given the recent bull run witnessed in the crypto market, you might be tempted to allocate a large portion of your wealth to cryptocurrencies. Do not do that. That's because your investment decisions will be governed by greed and fear, which in the end might lead to poor decisions. Allocate a reasonable portion to cryptos to ensure rational decisions.

Decide which crypto(s) you intend to invest in

As we have mentioned, there are over 5000 cryptocurrencies in the market. Unless you are a billionaire, it would be nearly impossible to invest in all of them, not to mention impractical. You should conduct proper due diligence on specific cryptos and settle on those that fit your investment criteria. Later, we will show you what to look out for a while selecting crypto to invest in.

Identify where to buy and the appropriate crypto wallet

There are several crypto exchanges where you can purchase nearly every crypto available. However, before selecting the platform to buy your cryptos, you should do market research and determine the fair price of the cryptos you intend to buy. We have reviewed the most reliable crypto exchanges below.

Finally, you should decide on the most appropriate crypto wallet. This should entirely depend on your preferences and whether the wallets support the cryptos you buy. However, if you intend to hold cryptos for a long time, we advise keeping them in cold storage where you have complete control of your private keys.

Brace for turbulent times where choppy markets will test your patience and possibly sanity. You should also prepare to up your investment in cryptos when you have more extra income or believe the cryptos are highly undervalued. This is how legendary investors accumulate their holdings.

4.4 Most Reliable Crypto Exchanges

We've already discussed the roles and types of crypto exchanges. We acknowledge that there are hundreds of crypto exchanges in the markets. Here's our review of the top five most reliable crypto exchanges.

1. Coinbase

Coinbase was established in 2012 by Brian Armstrong and Fred Ehrsam, making it one of the oldest crypto exchanges, and is operational in over 100 countries globally. Although Coinbase is strictly designed for cryptocurrencies, it offers multiple services to its clients. The services offered by Coinbase include Coinbase brokerage service, crypto trading services via Coinbase Pro, Coinbase wallet, and Coinbase merchant solutions. We will discuss these services later in this article.

It adheres to very strict money transmission and e-money regulatory compliance from top financial sector regulators globally. The US adhered to the Bank Secrecy Act, the USA Patriot Act, and money transmission laws in every state and is registered as a Money Services Business with FinCEN. Authorized by the Financial Conduct Authority (FCA) in the UK under the Electronic Money Regulations 2011 (FRN: 900635). Coinbase has a strict know your customer (KYC) verification policy.

This exchange uses both secure online and offline servers to secure its clients' digital currency from hackers. 98% of the customers' digital currency are held in "cold storage," i.e., secure offline servers away from prying hackers. The remaining 2% is held in secure online servers to ensure that its customers' liquidity needs are met. It has commercial, criminal insurance for an amount greater than the 2% held in online servers.

Customer balances are stored in custodial accounts with US banks or invested liquid money market securities in compliance with money transmitter laws.

As of March 2021, Coinbase supports over 500 cryptocurrencies, although there are only 42 tradable assets available. You can buy, deposit, send, receive, and withdraw these cryptos from their Coinbase or Coinbase Pro accounts.

The tradable cryptos include REN, ALGO, REP, AAVE, NU, ETC, ATOM, YFI, WBTC, XTZ, GNT, MANA, SNX, BTC, OMG, OXT, LTC, BAL, FIL, MKR, ETH, KNC, BSV, LRC, BNT, BAND, CVC, ZRX, UMA, UNI, EOS, BCH, Celo (CGLD), COMP, NMR, XRP, XLM, LINK, LOOM, ZEC, BAT, DNT, DASH, DAI, GRT, and USDC.

Coinbase charges a spread of 0.5% for fiat to crypto trades and 1% for crypto-to-crypto trades. Deposit of cryptos is unlimited, while deposit for fiat currencies is limited depending on the payment method. Withdrawals are limited to a maximum of $25,000. It has a minimum deposit of $1000 when you transfer fiat currency via SWIFT. You can deposit and withdraw via PayPal, debit card, credit card, wire transfer, ACH, SEPA transfer, or 3D Secure Card.

2. Binance

Binance is a third-party crypto exchange founded in 2017 by Changpeng Zhao and is headquartered in the European Isle of Malta. In about three of being operational, Binance has become one of the top crypto exchanges globally.

The popularity of Binance stems from the fact that it is the only crypto exchange with the highest ICO listings. It also offers the lowest trading fees of 0.1% for all tradable assets. When you trade more than $150000 a month, Binance can cut your trading fee to 0.02%. Using Binance coin (BNB) when paying the transaction fees allows you up to 25% discount, meaning the fees chargeable can be as low as 0.075%.

The platform supports 16 international languages, which ensures everyone is catered globally. However, it is banned in the following countries: Cuba, Herzegovina, Iran, Sudan, South Sudan, Syria, Venezuela, Yemen, Bosnia, Burma, Central African Republic, Belarus, Albania, Somalia, Syria, North Korea, Côte D'Ivoire, Kosovo, Lebanon, Liberia,

Ukraine, Croatia, and Zimbabwe. Note that traders can bypass the geo-blocking of IP addresses by using any VPN.

Finance has FDIC insurance coverage for deposits in USD up to $250,000.

3. Kraken

Kraken is one of the oldest crypto exchanges. It was established in 2011 by Jesse Powell but began operations in 2013. It has more than 62 tradable cryptos and accepts fiat currencies in USD, EUR, AUD, JPY, CAD, GBP, and CHF. The platform supports withdrawals by SWIFT, SEPA, domestic, and wire transfers, making it beginner friendly. It also offers very low fees ranging between 0% and 0.26% on every trade executed. However, dark pool fees can be as high as 0.36% per trade.

Kraken is banned in the following countries Afghanistan, Congo-Brazzaville, Congo-Kinshasa, Cuba, Iran, Iraq, Libya, North Korea, Syria, and Tajikistan. Its services are limited in these countries Central African Republic, Eritrea, Guinea-Bissau,

Lebanon, Mali, Namibia, Somalia, South Sudan, Sudan, and Yemen.

4. Bitfinex

Bitfinex was established in 2012 and is owned by iFinex Inc., headquartered in Hong Kong and registered in the British Virgin Islands. It is one of the most interesting crypto exchanges since it provides peer-to-peer (P2P) financing and an OTC market. This is advantageous for large trade orders executed in the OTC market, don't attract trading fees. On the main platform, fees can go as high as 0.2%. Other services offered by Bitfinex include derivatives trading, margin trading, and staking and lending.

When making bank deposits and withdrawals, you are charged a 0.1% fee. For expedited withdrawals, you will incur a 1% fee on the amount being withdrawn. This crypto exchange allows fiat deposits in EUR, JPY, GBP, and USD. Crypto deposits and withdrawals are cheaper. There are no limits on deposits and withdrawals. However, crypto withdrawals may take up to 12 hours.

Bitfinex holds only 0.5% of clients' funds online for liquidity purposes; the rest is held in cold storages. This came in the wake of the 2016 security breach, resulting in the loss of $72 million worth of Bitcoin. Bitfinex is banned in the US, Bangladesh, Kyrgyzstan, Ecuador, and Bolivia.

5. Huobi Global

Huobi Global crypto exchange began operations in 2013 and has headquarters in Singapore, Australia, China, Indonesia, Russia, Argentina, Japan, South Korea, and Thailand. It has over 340 tradable crypto assets. Trading fees on Huobi are much lower than the industry average. The maker fees average at 0.02% and 0.04% to 0.05% for taker fees.

Huobi has a robust consumer protection program. Apart from strong cybersecurity defence systems, it has put in place risk management measures. They include storing 98% of client funds in cold storages. It also has a User Protection Fund Initiative which holds 20% of all company revenue. This fund is intended to compensate clients in the unlikely event of hacking breaches or other non-trading losses.

Users can fund their accounts via ACH, credit cards, debit cards, wire transfer, or crypto. However, the exchange doesn't support the deposit or withdrawal of fiat currencies.

How to select the Best Crypto Exchange?

Several factors go into choosing the top crypto exchanges. They include the daily traded volume, the number of cryptocurrencies supported by the exchange, the exchange's average liquidity, and the number of markets the exchange legally operates in. Here's a list of the top 20 crypto exchanges based on these categories as of March 2021.

Top 20 Crypto Exchange by Liquidity

#	Name	Volume(24h)	Avg. Liquidity	# Markets	# Coins
1	Venus	$ 29,532,073,6 35	--	17	33
2	Binance	$ 29,141,777,5 37	621	110 4	33 9
3	HBTC	$ 10,265,891,9 00	316	155	11 6
4	ZG.com	$ 10,166,575,9 51	118	42	38
5	Hydax Exchang e	$8,044,491,1 99	299	80	44
6	Dsdaq	$8,026,945,6 71	298	59	46

7	Xtheta Global	$7,720,077,406	271	70	41
8	Mexo Exchange	$7,198,328,673	292	47	30
9	Huobi Global	$7,117,129,409	559	930	314
10	Upbit	$7,072,681,394	276	248	167
11	Hotcoin Global	$7,049,350,786	175	66	54
12	Bidesk	$6,692,350,249	275	63	35
13	VCC Exchange	$6,087,383,504	--	210	117

1 4	BitZ	$5,562,097,3 30	150	128	10 0
1 5	OKEx	$5,433,455,7 30	440	683	23 9
1 6	ZT	$5,160,650,0 45	164	75	61
1 7	BiONE	$5,108,386,6 67	181	209	15 7
1 8	RightBT C	$4,567,038,2 26	28	49	26
1 9	Ecxx	$4,318,336,8 27	162	17	8
2 0	IDCM	$4,226,929,0 12	--	25	21

Top 20 Crypto Exchange by number of markets served

#	Name	# Markets	Exchange Score	Volume(24h)	Avg. Liquidity	# Coins	Fiat Supported
1	Hotbit	1268	3.8	$51,791,124	199	694	--
2	Binance	1104	9.6	$29,141,777,537	621	339	AED, ARS, AUD
3	HitBTC	967	4.5	$2,941,488,271	417	441	--
4	Huobi Global	930	8.2	$7,117,129,409	559	314	--
5	Gate.io	914	6.6	$493,752,569	354	483	--
6	ProBit Exchange	801	5.8	$199,474,141	119	438	KRW

7	OKEx	6 83	6.9	$5,433,4 55,730	4 40	2 39	--
8	Bittre x	6 51	7.6	$267,59 7,942	3 12	3 28	US D
9	KuCoi n	6 11	8.2	$843,43 5,492	4 50	2 80	T OKE N
1 0	Huobi Kore a	5 74	6.1	$88,957, 080	4 88	2 24	KR W
1 1	Bilax y	5 49	3.8	$602,67 2,530	1 94	5 16	--
1 2	Crex 24	4 41	3.8	$3,452,2 28	4 4	3 75	--
1 3	MXC. COM	4 35	4.2	$686,95 5,354	2 88	3 39	--
1 4	Merc atox	4 11	3.3	$29,267, 339	2 6	2 37	--
1 5	Hoo	4 00	4.1	$1,135,3 64,985	2 95	3 32	--
1 6	YoBit	3 95	3.1	$21,366, 556	4 0	2 82	--

1 7	CoinE x	3 81	5	$210,57 4,697	1 78	1 78	--
1 8	FTX	3 80	--	$795,01 7,877	--	1 91	US D, EUR, GBP
1 9	CoinD CX	3 74	5.8	$22,616, 902	5 60	2 09	IN R
2 0	VinD AX	3 48	--	$281,27 8,747	--	1 78	--

Top 20 Crypto Exchange by number of cryptos supported

#	Nam e	# Coi ns	Exch ange Score	Volume(24h)	Avg . Liqu idity	# Mar kets	Fiat Supp orted
1	Hotbi t	6 94	3.8	$51,791, 124	1 99	1 268	--

2	Bilaxy	5 16	3.8	$602,672,530	1 94	5 49	--
3	Gate.io	4 83	6.6	$493,752,569	3 54	9 14	--
4	HitBTC	4 41	4.5	$2,941,488,271	4 17	9 67	--
5	ProBit Exchange	4 38	5.8	$199,474,141	1 19	8 01	KRW
6	Crex 24	3 75	3.8	$3,452,228	4 4	4 41	--
7	Binance	3 39	9.6	$29,141,777,537	6 21	1 104	AED, ARS, AUD
8	MXC.COM	3 39	4.2	$686,955,354	2 88	4 35	--

9	Hoo	3 32	4.1	$1,135,3 64,985	2 95	4 00	--
1 0	Bittre x	3 28	7.6	$267,59 7,942	3 12	6 51	USD
1 1	Huobi Glob al	3 14	8.2	$7,117,1 29,409	5 59	9 30	--
1 2	YoBit	2 82	3.1	$ 21,366,5 56	4 0	3 95	--
1 3	KuCoi n	2 80	8.2	$843,43 5,492	4 50	6 11	TOKE N
1 4	OKEx	2 39	6.9	$5,433,4 55,730	4 40	6 83	--
1 5	Merc atox	2 37	3.3	$29,267, 339	2 6	4 11	--

1 6	Bithu mb Glob al	2 26	5.5	$168,17 8,143	9 1	2 98	RUB, TRY
1 7	Huobi Kore a	2 24	6.1	$ 88,957,0 80	4 88	5 74	KRW
1 8	STEX	2 13	3.2	$24,043, 781	3 4	2 80	--
1 9	CoinD CX	2 09	5.8	$22,616, 902	5 60	3 74	INR
2 0	FTX	1 91	--	$795,01 7,877	--	3 80	USD, EUR, GBP

Top 20 Crypto Exchange by Average Liquidity

#	Name	Avg. Liquidity	Exchange Score	Volume(24h)	# Markets	# Coins	Fiat Supported
1	Folgory	736	3.9	$306,621,048	228	90	--
2	Binance	621	9.6	$29,141,777,537	1104	339	AED, ARS, AUD
3	CoinDCX	560	5.8	$22,616,902	374	209	INR
4	Huobi Global	559	8.2	$7,117,129,409	930	314	--
5	Huobi Indonesia	531	4.7	$505,436	98	75	IDR
6	Kraken	521	8.6	$1,594,554,468	284	62	USD,

7	Huobi Korea	4 88	6.1	$88,957,080	5 74	2 24	KR W
8	Coinbase Pro	4 86	8.9	$3,196,209,640	1 42	4 6	US D, EUR, GBP
9	Bitfinex	4 82	8.4	$1,091,268,044	2 73	1 44	US D, EUR, GBP
1 0	IndoEx	4 77	3.8	$2,662,575,105	1 65	4 8	--
1 1	Bitrue	4 68	4.4	$787,861,322	2 06	9 8	--
1 2	PayBito	4 65	3.3	$1,124,933,691	5 1	1 7	US D
1 3	KuCoin	4 50	8.2	$843,435,492	6 11	2 80	TOKE N

1 4	OKEx	4 40	6.9	$5,433,4 55,730	6 83	2 39	--
1 5	Bitcoi n.com Excha nge	4 27	3.9	$2,568,3 22,427	1 51	7 2	--
1 6	Chan gelly PRO	4 27	3.2	$2,430,3 28,068	9 1	3 4	--
1 7	HitBT C	4 17	4.5	$2,941,4 88,271	9 67	4 41	--
1 8	LATO KEN	4 12	4.2	$293,16 1,251	2 71	1 55	--
1 9	XT	4 00	4.8	$1,158,1 80,252	1 34	9 8	--
2 0	Coina ll	3 86	3.3	$4,028,8 94	1 34	8 7	--

4.5 What Should You Know Before Investing in Cryptos?

You might be ready to start your journey investing in cryptos. At this point, you are already familiar with crypto wallets, crypto exchanges, and you are aware of the significant cryptos in the market. However, here are a few things you should know before investing in cryptos:

Avoid the hype!

When it comes to investing, it is not a good idea to jump into the buying frenzy. Fear of missing out (FOMO) could end up being the difference between you picking winning crypto to invest in and sticking with joke crypto. We live in the age of sensational media headlines, which may seem like a call to action. Whenever you see such sensational headlines, master all the courage you can to avoid falling into the FOMO rabbit hole.

We have witnessed random cryptos being pumped by celebrities to capture global media attention as an investment-worthy token, only for them to end up being utter scams. The problem with such media hype is that the value of the cryptos tends to be overvalued. Whenever you see an unknown cryptocurrency being hyped, be cautious, especially if such tokens aren't proven in the DeFi community. They could be a run-of-the-mill pump and dump scams. This is when crypto is hyped by those who own them to inflate the price. Once people start buying, and the price goes up, they sell their cryptos in the market, leaving unsuspecting investors with dud cryptos and massive losses.

Consider Staking your cryptos

Crypto Staking is an alternative to crypto mining. As a crypto investor, you intend to hold your portfolio for a longer period, i.e., HODLing. While your portfolio might appreciate in the long run, you should also consider staking your cryptos. That way, you will earn interest instead of your crypto lying around idly. Consider staking as some sort of 'value addition' tactic.

Staking is one of the easiest ways for you to earn periodic income passively. Since the advent of the

Proof-of-Stake (PoS) consensus mechanism, crypto holders can lock up their cryptos in a smart contract which can then be used to verify the transaction in a blockchain. In this case, stakers are the validators on the network. When you validate transactions on the network, the network rewards you – often in cryptos. This presents an easy way to earn passive income while still maintaining your crypto portfolio. More so, some crypto wallets allow you to stake your cryptos directly. You can also stake from crypto exchanges like Binance.

Note that not all cryptos can be staked. If you intend to stake, you should consider investing in cryptos that can be staked.

Consider crypto lending

Crypto lending is also an ideal way of earning passive income while maintaining your crypto portfolio. You can earn interest by lending your cryptos via several crypto lending platforms or crypto exchanges. Crypto lending has become rampant with the growth of crypto derivatives. Leveraged traders need to borrow cryptos for trading. These cryptos are often lent by spot investors who are compensated through daily interests. This way, your portfolio earns interest while you hold for the long haul.

Be wary of ICOs

Initial coin offerings (ICOs) have become the most common method by which new cryptos are introduced into the market. While there have been some successful ICOs in the past, namely Ethereum, most scammers use ICOs as their weapon of choice. The quickest way of spotting a scam ICO is if you are promised: "guaranteed returns" on your investment. When it comes to cryptos, there is no such thing as a guaranteed return on investment. If you are new to cryptocurrencies, you are better off investing in mainstream cryptos – avoid ICOs.

Look out for the utility of the crypto

We cannot stress this enough. If you are new to cryptos, you are better off investing in well-established and mainstream cryptos. We covered the most important cryptos in 'Session 2'. If you'd want to invest in something exotic, then you better be ready to do some serious due diligence.

Take Ethereum, for example. Its massive success can be attributed to its contribution to the kick-starting and furthering development of decentralized finance. Ethereum gave crypto developers globally a platform to build their own decentralized applications. Ethereum gave us smart contracts! By some measure, every altcoin brings some utility to the DeFi ecosystem. For example, the crypto community is continually addressing problems with scalability, absolute privacy, and interoperability. These issues can be used as a yardstick to measure the usefulness of an altcoin. If it doesn't address at least one of them, then do not bother investing. Chances are, you'll be parking your fund in dud crypto.

Session 5
Getting Started with Crypto Trading

5.1 What is Crypto Trading?

Crypto trading involves buying or selling cryptocurrencies over the short term – i.e., going long or short. Trading focusses on maximizing short-term gains by taking advantage of volatility and media hype. Traders often spend most of their time observing chart patterns and analyzing trends before deciding whether to go short or long.

Most traders also use proprietary tools and techniques to enhance their profits. They also take advantage of the various order types to help them open and close positions under specific market conditions. Risk management techniques such as the use of leverage and stop-loss levels are also handy to traders.

In a nutshell, traders aim to profit in the market by taking advantage of short-term volatility. Primarily, most traders use leverage to increase the size of their positions and magnify their potential profits. More so, traders often prefer to trade contract for difference (CFD) assets than own the underlying assets.

5.2 Introduction to Cryptocurrency Trading

In the contemporary sense, crypto trading often implies trading crypto CFDs. Typically, most crypto traders do not own the underlying cryptos but merely speculate on the direction that the crypto's price will take. Before we dive deeper into crypto trading, there are several terminologies that you will encounter in the course of trading. We devote this section to explaining the basic terminologies involve in crypto trading.

The contract for difference (CFD): These are crypto derivatives that help you speculate on a crypto price without owning the underlying crypto. That means you can go long (buy) if you believe that the crypto will appreciate and short (sell) when you believe that the price will drop. CFDs also enables crypto traders to use leverage.

Leverage: is also called margin. Leverage is a credit facility extended to you by your broker, which helps you increase your exposure to a particular asset. For example, if you take leverage of 100x, you will open a position that is 100x the size of your account deposit. Say you have a $1000 deposit in your account. With a leverage of 100x, you can open a position worth $100,000. Note that leverage can only be used when trading derivatives. It significantly increases your potential profits but also makes the downside huge.

Currency pairs: In crypto trading, tradable assets are in the form of currency pairs. For example, BTC/USD. The price of a currency pair shows how much of the quote currency is needed to buy one unit of the base currency. Let's say that the price of BTC/ETH is $1000. This means that you will need 1000 USD to buy 1 BTC.

Base Currency: This is the first currency that appears on a currency pair. In the currency pair BTC/ETH, BTC is the base currency.

Quote currency: This is the second currency that appears in a currency pair. In the above example, ETH is the quote currency.

Going long: This means buying a currency pair. Typically, traders go long when they believe that the price of a currency pair will increase. More technically, it means that the base currency will become stronger than the quote currency or that the quote currency will become weaker than the base currency.

Short selling: This means selling a currency pair. Traders 'short sell' when they believe that the price of the currency pair will drop. This implies that the base currency will become weaker than the quote currency or that the quote currency will become stronger than the base currency.

Crypto trading: As we have mentioned, trading involves either going long or short. When you go long, it means that you are selling the quote currency to buy the base currency since you believe that the price of the currency pair will increase. Going short means selling the base currency to buy the quote currency since you believe that the price of the currency pair will drop.

Bid price: This is the price that your broker will demand when you buy a currency pair

Ask price: This is the price that your broker will pay when you sell a currency pair, i.e., when going short.

Spread: this is the difference between the bid price and the ask price. It is commonly referred to as bid/ask spread. The spread is primarily how most brokers earn their revenue. Note that the spread is often considered a cost to the trader; thus, always select the broker who offers you the least spread.

Liquidity: this refers to the trading activity in a particular market. High liquidity means that there is a high trading volume in the market with many participants on either side of the trade. In this case, there are many sellers and a lot of buyers in the market for that particular currency pair. Low liquidity means that there are few buyers and sellers active in the market.

Volatility: this refers to the unpredictable and rapid fluctuation of the price of a currency pair. High volatility means that a particular currency pair's price fluctuates rapidly and unpredictably during a trading session. Low volatility means that the price has low fluctuations and follows a particular trend.

Slippage: This is the difference between the price that you request a broker to execute your trade and the price that the trade is executed. Slippages occur when the price of a currency pair changes from when you place an order to when that order is executed. The main causes of slippage in crypto trading are market volatility and latency in your broker's trade execution speed.

Maker: This is a trader who provides liquidity to the market, i.e., makes liquidity. They are often rewarded with a maker fee

Taker: These are traders who are buying from the crypto market, i.e., taking liquidity from the market. In crypto trading, takers are charged a fee.

Order book: is a list of all open trades in the market, showing the buy and sell orders present in the market, along with their corresponding prices. Order books play an important role in the price discovery of a currency pair.

5.3 Different Order Types

In crypto trading, an order is an instruction you give your broker or market intermediary to perform a particular transaction on your behalf. This may either be to sell to buy a particular currency pair or close a particular position.

Primarily, there are two order types: market and pending orders.

Market Orders

This is an instruction to your broker to execute that specified trade instantly based on the prevailing market price. Depending on the type of trade you are executing, your order will be executed at either the bid or the ask price. If you are buying a currency pair, your trade will be executed at the 'ask price', and if you are short selling, the trade will be executed at the 'bid price'.

Market orders are the most common types of orders among traders. That is because the trades are often executed at the best price possible and instantly. However, the trader may not have full control of the market price since slippages may occur, resulting in their trade being executed at a different price than they requested.

Pending Orders

These are orders instructing your broker or market intermediary to execute your specified trade in the future when the price of a particular asset reaches a specific level. These orders can then only be executed when the pre-set market conditions are met. Such orders are ideal for traders who do not have the time to continually monitor the market to find ideal entry and exit points.

Pending orders are categorized into limit orders and stop orders.

Limit Orders

These are orders to execute a particular trade at a specified price or better. However, due to market fluctuations, the specified price may not be attained, meaning that the order may not be filled. If the specified price is reached, the order will always be filled at a price better than expected by the trader. This is one of the main advantages of limit orders. It helps traders avoid slippages and have their trades executed at specific prices or, better, enhancing profits.

Limit orders are further categorized into buy limit and sell limit orders.

Buy limit order: This is an order to execute a long trade when the price of an asset reaches a specified level that is lower than the current market price.

Sell limit order is the opposite of the buy limit order. Using this order instructs your broker to sell a particular currency pair when its price reaches a specified level that is higher than the current market price.

Note that if the specified price is not reached, your trade will not be executed.

Stop Orders: These are pending orders which instruct your broker to buy or sell a particular currency pair when its price reaches a specified level. The difference between limit orders and stop orders is that your trade will be executed at the exact specified price or a better one with limit orders. Your trade is executed at the best available price for stop orders once the asset hits the target price. This is the similarity between stop orders and market orders – they are both filled at the best available price, which could be a little lower or higher than the specified price. You could say that the stop order becomes a market order once the pre-determined price is reached.

Stop orders are categorized into buy stop orders and sell stop orders.

Buy stop orders: this is an instruction for your broker to buy a particular currency pair once the price of an asset reaches a specified price higher than the current market price. This means that when the price of the currency pair hits the pre-determined price, a long trade will be executed at the best available price. The target price is called the buy stop price.

Sell stop order: this is the opposite of the buy stop order. It is an instruction for your broker to short sell a particular currency pair when its price reaches a target price that is lower than the current market price. Once the sell stop price is reached, the sell order will be executed at the best available price.

Similar to the limit orders, the stop orders will not be executed is the currency pair doesn't reach the target price.

Stop limit orders: This is a combination of the limit and stop orders. Such orders are meant to increase the precision of the price at which trades are executed. The stop limit orders are similar to the stop orders, only that instead of the trade being filled at the best available price, it is converted into a limit order. This way, once the price reaches the pre-determined level, your trade will be executed at the exact price or a better one instead of being executed at the best available price.

Stop limit orders are categorized into buy stop limit and sell stop limit orders.

Buy stop limit order: this is an instruction for your broker to buy a particular currency pair once the price of an asset reaches a specified price higher than the current market price. This means that when the price of the currency pair hits the pre-determined price, a long trade will be executed at the specified price or better instead of being converted into a market order.

Sell stop limit order: this is the opposite of the buy stop order. It is an instruction for your broker to short sell a particular currency pair when its price reaches a target price that is lower than the current market price. Once the sell stop price is reached, the sell order will be executed at the specified target price or better, instead of being converted into a market order.

Take Profit orders: These are orders to your broker to close an open position when the price reaches a specified level above the entry-level for a buy order and lower than the entry price for a short position. Take profit orders can also be modified into limit orders.

172

Take profit limit orders: These are a modification to the take profit order. They are used to close an open position at the specified take profit level and trigger a limit order simultaneously. Therefore, it involves closing one position and opening another.

The take profit limit order has two sets of prices. Firstly, the profit price is used to close a position when the currency pair touches it. Secondly, it has a limit price, which is used to trigger the limit order. Remember that a limit order is often executed at the limit price or better.

The take profit limit orders are further subdivided into two categories – buy take profit limit orders and sell take profit limit orders.

Buy take profit limit order: This order often corresponds with closing out a short position. As we discussed above, a buy limit order is an order to execute a long trade when the price of an asset reaches a specified level that is lower than the current market price.

When setting the take profit order for a short position, the target price is set lower than the market price since you expect the price of the currency pair to drop when you open a short position.

Sell take profit limit order: This order corresponds to closing a long position. We mentioned earlier that a sell limit order instructs your broker to sell a particular currency pair when it price reaches a specified level that is higher than the current market price.

For a long position, the take profit level is set above the current market price. This is because when buying a currency pair, you do so, hoping the price will increase.

Stop Loss Orders

As the name suggests, these are designed to limit a trader's downside. They are meant to close out a position if the market trends in the opposite direction. For example, if you open a short position, you hope that the price will drop. Instead, if the currency pair rises, it means that you are accruing losses on your trading account. If these loses continue, your account could be wiped out. However, setting a stop loss order lets you instruct your broker to automatically close your position after the losses in your trading account reach a specific level. The stop-loss orders can be modified into buy stop loss orders and sell stop loss orders. These orders are used to open positions where market breakouts occur.

Buy stop loss orders: These orders are similar to the buy stop orders. They correspond to a stop loss order for a short position. Remember that the stop-loss for a short position is placed above the market price. For the buy stop loss orders, two prices are set – the stop-loss price and the price at which the buy stop loss order will be triggered. Note that this order triggers the execution of a long position at the best available price.

The logic behind the buy stop loss orders is that if the stop-loss for a short position is triggered, the market is adopting a bullish trend.

Sell stop loss orders: These orders are similar to sell stop orders. They correspond to the stop-loss order for a long position. Remember that when you buy a currency pair, you place the stop-loss below the market price to protect you if the market adopts a downtrend. If the market turns bearish, the sell stop loss order will be triggered, and a short position will be executed.

In this case, when the stop-loss for a long position is triggered, it means that the market is adopting a bearish trend.

Stop Loss limit orders

These are also a variation of the stop loss. They convert the stop loss price into the price for a limit order. This means that to convert a stop loss into a stop loss limit order, you must have two inputs. Firstly, the stop price will trigger the close of an open position and a limit price.

The stop loss limit orders can be categorized into buy stop loss limit orders and sell stop loss limit orders.

Buy stop loss limit-order corresponds to the stop loss of a short-sell position. These orders work the same way as buy stop limit orders. Remember, we discussed earlier that a buy stop limit order is an instruction for your broker to buy a particular currency pair once the price of an asset reaches a specified price higher than the current market price.

In this case, however, you will use the stop loss price for a short position to execute a long trade. When the stop loss is triggered, and your position is closed, a long position will be opened at the exact stop loss price or better.

Sell stop loss limit order: This order corresponds with the stop loss price for a buy order, and they work similarly to the sell stop limit orders. Remember that the sell stop limit order is an instruction for your broker to short-sell a particular currency pair when its price reaches a lower target price than the current market price. Once the stop loss level for a long trade is triggered, the sell order will be executed at the specified target price or better.

There is no guarantee that your trade will be executed with all these pending order types, especially where there is slippage in the market. Therefore, it is prudent to set the pending orders slightly lower than the take profit level or the stop loss price. This increases their likelihood of being executed.

Trailing Stop Orders

This order is a modification of the buy stop and the sell stop orders. Note that the difference with this order is that it isn't used to open positions but for risk management purposes. This order is used to mitigate significant loses in an already opened position.

Trailing stop orders are often attached to some pips below the prevailing market price. This means that when the price rises in an open position and your profits accumulate, the trailing stop also rises along with it. When the trend changes and the market adopt a bearish trend, your position will be close when the market price reaches the trailing stop level.

For an open short position, the trailing stop is placed specific points above the market price. As the downtrend continues, the trailing stop will continue moving downwards. This ensures that your profits are secured if the market reverses into a bullish trend.

Trailing Stop Limit orders: You can also use the trailing stop to set a trigger price or a limit order. In this case, the trailing stop limit orders will combine the characteristics of the trailing stop and the stop limit. Remember that you can have it trail the market price by a percentage or a fixed dollar amount when setting the trailing stop. Thus, when the market trend reverses and hits the trailing stop price, the trailing stop limit order will be triggered.

When setting up the trailing stop limit order, three inputs are necessary:

- The trailing stop amount or percentage
- The stop price, which when hit by the market, will trigger the trailing stop limit order
- The limit price which your order will be executed at. Note that your order will be executed at the limit price or better

For this order, the trail is the amount by which the market must pull back for the trailing stop limit order is triggered.

Conditional Order Types

Good for Day Order: This order will remain valid until the day ends. If the conditions for triggering the order aren't met within that trading day, the pending order is automatically cancelled.

Good till Day Order: This type of order can remain active for some specified number of days, after which they are cancelled.

Immediate or Cancel Order (IOC): This conditional order stipulates that as much volume as possible must be filled for a particular trade, and any unfilled amount is cancelled. For example, if your order is for 10 BTC but only get 8 BTC, then the remaining 2 BTC is cancelled.

Fill or kill (FOK)/ All or none orders: These orders require that the entire order amount is executed or cancelled. For example, if your trade is a FOK order for 10 BTC, if there is no 10 BTC in the market at that time, the entire order is cancelled. Even if only 9 BTC is available, the order will still be cancelled.

Iceberg / Hidden Orders: These orders serve to divide a significantly large order size into smaller orders submitted to the market independently as limit orders. Such orders hide large order quantities to avoid distorting the market price.

One cancels the other (OCO) orders: These orders are submitted to the market in pairs. They are either competing or opposing orders. Thus, when one order is filled, the other one is automatically cancelled.

One sends the other (OSO) orders: These are orders which, when one is closed, another one is triggered. They are also called conditional close orders. The best examples are the take profit limit orders.

One cancels all (OCA) orders: This type of order allows traders to program multiple unrelated orders such that when one order is filled, all the others are automatically cancelled. This order helps traders who have limited trading budgets and cannot afford to open multiple positions.

Post limit / Post only orders: In crypto trading, traders use these orders to ensure that their buy or sell orders are filled under 'maker' and 'taker' as appropriate.

5.4 Fundamental and Sentimental Analysis

Fundamental and sentimental analysis is vital for any crypto trader. Remember, we mentioned earlier that their demand in the market determines the value of cryptos. In turn, demand is driven by the inherent usefulness of the crypto, determined by fundamental analysis, and what people are willing to pay for it, determined by sentimental analysis. Thus, both fundamental and sentimental analyses play a crucial role in finding the best possible crypto to trade or invest.

Fundamental Analysis

Fundamental analysis is also called qualitative analysis. This is a subjective judgment based on non-quantifiable information, such as management expertise, industry cycles, the strength of research and development and labor relations.

The qualitative analysis contrasts with Quantitative analysis, which focuses on numbers found in reports such as balance sheets. However, the two techniques will often be used together to examine a company's operations and evaluate its potential as an investment opportunity.

Fundamental analysis attempts to measure an asset or cryptocurrency's intrinsic value by examining related economic and financial factors, which can be both qualitative and quantitative.

Fundamental analysts' study anything that can affect the value, including macro-economic factors and micro-economic. The end goal of fundamental analysis is to produce a quantitative value that an investor can compare with the digital asset's current price, indicating whether the asset is undervalued or overvalued.

Fundamental analysis is primarily a SWOT analysis of a particular cryptocurrency. Due to their nature, traditional types of fundamental analyses won't work with cryptos. This is because cryptos might add billions in value overnight. The fundamental analysis of a cryptocurrency involves three aspects:

- The project, i.e., the intended purpose of the crypto
- Competition from other cryptos

- The validity of its real-world application

The Crypto's Project

You should note that cryptos are often designed to solve a specific goal. To determine the usefulness of crypto, you should get rad through its whitepaper and determine what exactly it aims to solve. This will help avoid scam cryptos designed to pump up prices so that the founders can dump them, leaving investors and traders with useless cryptos. Note that the inherent value is often what other people are willing to pay for it. If everyone knows that particular crypto is worthless, you can expect that its price will tank.

To determine this, you should also dig into the original team that developed the crypto. It would be best if you took a clue from the top cryptos in the market; their founders are almost geniuses with PHDs in quantitative fields. They have impressive academic and practical careers with ground-breaking projects under their belt. When the crypto team is open about their experiences and their credentials can be verified, this should be considered a plus. However, if you cannot independently verify their credentials, take this as a red flag and abandon any interest you have in that crypto.

Next, try to ascertain if the cryptos project is relevant or even required at all. Presently, over 5000 altcoins are circulating in the crypto market. There are so many privacy clones, PoS projects, 'DAPPs' projects (biggest meme of them all), 'fast transaction' based cryptocurrency and so on. The top 100 is overcrowded and full of similar ideas, and I believe 80% of them will eventually die. If you randomly selected 50 cryptos from the top 100 cryptos – it doesn't matter the criteria you use to rank them – you will notice that most of them aim to solve the same thing. There is very little differentiation. Now try to do this with the top 2000 cryptos; you will notice that the market if full of copycats, a lot of which will die out.

When conducting your fundamental analysis, the primary goal is to establish which crypto will survive in the long-term and which ones are on life support. It goes without saying that you should only trade or invest in those with higher chances of being around in the longer term.

To summarize this point, the project means identifying what exactly is the project trying to achieve. Legitimate cryptos have official websites which provide the public with this information. More so, they must have a whitepaper that describes the project to a layperson.

What I have observed is, most people tend to skip any mention of technology/algo/implementation, thinking 'I do not have a technical background', and this is where some get it wrong. It is a no-brainer that viable crypto should aspire and have believable chances of solving a real-world problem. If this is not the case, then do not consider it. A crypto project has to solve a real-world problem, a problem with the blockchain technology itself, or improvise upon an existing idea by a big margin.

Competition from other cryptos

As we have mentioned above, there are over 5000 cryptos in the market, and all of them are trying to solve a specific problem. Most of them are arguably designed to solve a similar problem either in the real world or a problem existing in the blockchain

186

technology itself. The problem is where most of them have duplicated each other's roles and don't seem to have any value addition. In this case, you have to ask yourself which duplicate cryptos have a better chance of survival?

Having similar roles is not the problem here. The problem seems to stem from identifying marginally better cryptos. Remember that crypto doesn't just have a singular role. It could have multiple roles and be significantly better at these roles than others. Most fundamental analyses are always inclined to bet on low/micro-cap projects aiming to take on the more established ones and envision to take the innovation to the next level.

Competition is not always a bad thing. It encourages innovation among the competitors while the one which cannot adapt dies out. In cryptos, competition is where the survival of the fittest plays out. The success of a project also highly depends on the competition, market dynamics, and the community backing it.

Validity in the real-world application

As we have mentioned, crypto must have a purpose. It should just be for purely speculative purposes or to be used as a means of exchange. It has to have a specific real-world application. With the mainstream explosion of decentralized finance, it is important, now more than ever, that cryptos must have a real-world application. The fundamental analysis of cryptos is not farfetched. Fully decentralized organizations are at least several years away. But that doesn't mean that cryptos should not be attempting to further such goals. After all, every idea starts with just one step.

The end goal of every crypto should be revolutionizing at least one aspect of our daily lives. Take Bitcoin, for example. Its first real-world application was to ensure the decentralization of the monetary system. Ethereum's goal was to develop and nurture decentralized finance and provide a platform where DAPPs could thrive. Cryptos, like Monero, ensured total anonymity.

The point of this aspect of fundamental analysis is that every crypto must have an inherent functionality. The potential of blockchain technology is limitless. In the recent past, we have witnessed the migration of the traditional technology infrastructure of existing big companies to a decentralized one. This means that cryptos' functionality is shifting from being finance centered to aiding in revolutionizing the world as we know it.

Arguably, cryptocurrencies that are fundamentally strong in the long run are those which have this vision. Another approach is looking into the projects aiming to improve blockchain technology, say the projects improving and enhancing the Ethereum ecosystem, or bring innovation in the blockchain space, like STO focused projects.

Let's take a case study involving the rise of privacy coins.

Case study: The Rise of Privacy Coins

A privacy coin is a type of cryptocurrency that deliberately obfuscates a transactions link. This ensures that the wallet activity between the transacting parties remain anonymous and cannot be tracked. It becomes impossible to establish the transaction history or the funds that a particular wallet holds with cryptographic obscuring. The best privacy coins are Monero and Pirate Coin (ARRR).

How Privacy Coins Work?

Most cryptocurrencies like Bitcoin are not anonymous – they are pseudonymous. This means that a person's real identity is severed from their public wallet address. However, the transactions of a particular wallet are made public. That means you can view the amount of cryptocurrency held by a wallet and its transaction history. Note that it is not impossible to make the connection between a wallet address and your real-life identity. However, note that people can track your wallet along with every financial activity. Privacy coins like Monero and Pirate have solved this privacy problem by making cryptocurrency entirely private.

Monero

Monero (XMR) was launched in 2014. It uses 'Ring signatures' to cloak the sender's identity and the recipient of the crypto. When you initiate a transaction, a group of signers sign the transaction, which hides the actual sender's identity. Think of this as buying a gift for a colleague but having your entire office sign the card. This way, they won't know who bought the gift unless you tell them. In this case, if you send Monero to someone, they won't know you are the sender.

A Monero sender will generate a one-time 'spend key' that the recipient can only detect. The recipient is the only person who can spend the crypto using that key. Monero also uses stealth addresses which generates a one-time public key for recipients. It ensures that the fund being received is not directly connected to your wallet, but miners can verify that this transaction occurred, preventing the double-spending problem. More so, the Ring Confidential Transactions (RCT) masks the amount being sent and received. RCT is used as proof that Monero is not being used fraudulently. For example, if your wallet has 6 Monero and you only intend to send 2, you will have to send the whole balance of 5, then receive back 3.

Pirate (ARRR)

Pirate chain was created in 2018 and utilizes zk-SNARKs that 100% shields the peer-to-peer transactions on the blockchain. This makes all transaction with Pirate Chain completely anonymous and private.

The problem of double spending in the network is eliminated by using the Delayed Proof of Work (DPOW) concept. This concept also safeguards the Pirate Chain from 51% attacks using the Bitcoin blockchain as a backup for the ARRR. It means that if hackers wanted to attack the Pirate Chain, they would have first to attack Bitcoin – making it virtually impossible.

The Pirate Chain also implements the use of a block explorer. It ensures that observers can see the transactions on the platform but cannot see the senders and recipients' addresses. What's more, the code prevents any leakage of the transaction metadata from being made public.

Why use Privacy Coins?

The need for decentralization and absolute privacy precipitated the mainstream acceptance of cryptocurrencies in general. Blockchain technology has ensured anonymity and no external controls on the cryptos. Over time, cryptocurrencies have emerged as a viable store of value. This has been especially true in 2020 as the coronavirus pandemic ravaged the value of fiat currencies.

However, as we have noticed, most mainstream cryptocurrencies such as Bitcoin are not entirely private and anonymous. With the increasing mainstream penetration of DeFi, cryptocurrencies are becoming a daily part of financial transactions. Globally, counties are developing their version of cryptocurrencies, which won't be anonymous as well. Governments can't relinquish surveillance and the treasure trove that comes from financial data. We live in an age where information and data are being monetized and frequently weaponized. More so, with the increasing threat of authoritarian governments, absolute privacy is needed now, more than ever.

This is where Privacy coins thrive. They offer you the same blockchain advantages and store of value as other cryptocurrencies, but with an added advantage of absolute privacy. Privacy is a human right, and with Privacy Coins, your financial privacy is strictly yours. Decentralized finance (DeFi) is the without a doubt is the future of finance. With the increasing need for absolute privacy, cryptocurrencies like Bitcoin that do not offer absolute privacy are bound to be replaced. Privacy Coins such as Monero and Pirate could be the future of decentralized finance.

Sentimental Analysis

Sentimental analysis of cryptos is similar to fundamental analysis, only that it involves a more personal and subjective analysis of the public's opinion. In the long run, crypto investors might be unaffected by sentimental analysis. Crypto traders are the most impacted by the public's sentiment regarding particular crypto. It can be part of

Fundamental Analysis, but it is not the best form of determining real value.

It is unlikely that the fundamental aspects of a cryptocurrency are going to change in the short term. These factors include the real-world application of crypto, the problems that crypto aims to solve, or any significant changes among top crypto competitors. We have discussed these factors under the fundamental analysis section. The public's sentiment determines the daily fluctuation in the price of cryptocurrencies. In the short term, the mastery of sentimental analysis can be an invaluable tool for a crypto trader. However, properly implement sentimental analysis in crypto trading can be tedious and a painstaking process. But when done right, the reward is more than worth it.

In many finance trading guides, investors and traders are often advised to avoid making any trading or investment decisions based on emotions. This is only half true. When it comes to cryptocurrencies, your emotions may not matter, but other people's emotions regarding particular crypto are entirely valid.

We live in a digital era where contagion is the order of the day. To understand this, you have to remember that since cryptocurrencies have a limited supply, their price is driven by demand. This is where sentimental analysis comes in. when the public's sentiment about particular crypto is positive; there will be a surge in demand for that crypto which leads to the astronomical increase in prices — we will see this in a case study later on. Conversely, when the public's sentiment regarding particular crypto is negative, it will result in people dumping their cryptos in the market, which causes the price to drop. Thus, having your finger on the pulse of the public's sentiment can prove lucrative for a crypto trader in deciding whether to buy or particular short crypto.

One of the biggest causes of crypto volatility has always been sensational news headlines. Unlike other assets, cryptocurrencies have no fundamentals, so traders and investors cannot analyze financial statements to see how crypto performs. This means that the pricing of cryptocurrencies is entirely arbitrary and are based on market sentiment.

So, what exactly does sentimental analysis involve?

In the current age of globalization, information travels to the corners of the world in seconds. We are all digitally interconnected, which means that actionable intel can almost immediately be factored into the market. Sentimental analysis in crypto trading can be derived from news headlines or social media posts. It is hard to argue that most of our days are spent either glued to TV or browsing on social media. In the past couple of years, the volatility in cryptocurrencies can almost entirely be attributed to the media's sensational headlines. These headlines serve the function of polarizing traders who make irrational trading decisions out of the fear of missing out (FOMO).

Retail crypto traders form a significant portion of the crypto market, and they are the most active. This means that a large percentage of price fluctuations can be directly attributed to demand by retail traders. Here's where sentimental analysis comes in.

The average retail trader hardly does any thorough technical or fundamental analyzing of a given cryptocurrency. This is in contrast to institutional investors who take the due diligence process seriously. Before institutional investors take on a cryptocurrency on their portfolio, an astonishing amount of due diligence must first be done. The buy or sell decision for retail traders and investors is almost always purely made out of other traders and investors' recommendation. It is a crowding effect.

When a trader sees a sensational news article that mentions that other traders and investors are getting in on a particular crypto, they also jump in without due diligence. The public's sentiment creates a contagion that spreads throughout the market.

Sentimental Analysis case study

Bitcoin

For example, on February 8, 2021, Tesla announced that it had purchased BTC worth $1.5 billion. Within minutes, every media outlet had picked up the headline. Consequently, BTC gained about 14% in less than 90 minutes. Such sensational headlines drive up the demand for cryptocurrencies because association with reputable global organizations or celebrities increase their legitimacy.

As the adoption rate increases, so does the value since supply remains finite.

Such sensational headlines also create an irrational fear of missing out (FOMO). Cryptos became popular as a result of social contagion. An argument can be made that majority of retail crypto investors do not understand the concept of cryptocurrencies. Most people buy and sell because they see other people doing that, not because they understand the inherent properties of the value of cryptos.

That means when you see people buying cryptos; you also get in on the action so that you aren't left out.

The same goes when you notice headlines that people are selling.

Dogecoin

On February 4, 2021, Elon Musk made a series of tweets endorsing dogecoin, an obscure cryptocurrency. As a result, its price surge more than 50% within minutes of his tweets.

There are several indexes in the market which attempt to measure the sentiment in the crypto market. Such indexes take advantage of the fear and greed among retail traders. The basic idea behind such metrics is that traders are frequently guided by the Fear of Missing Out (FOMO).

5.5 Importance of Diversifying Your Crypto Portfolio

Diversifying your crypto portfolio means having different types of crypto in your portfolio. This follows the adage of not having all your eggs in one basket. You don't have to own every crypto in the market; this is impossible because there are over 5000 of them — most of which you will probably never hear about.

As is with any investment, it is wise to diversify your portfolio. While most people have been relying on Bitcoin trades and HODLing for the longest time, this exposes them to volatility and systemic risks. When you are overly reliant on one crypto, it means that your wealth is exposed to its volatility. A significant portion of this risk is eliminated through diversifying your portfolio.

Reasons for Diversification

Cryptocurrencies are inherently volatile. In the recent past, cryptocurrencies have been increasingly susceptible to sensational news headlines. Over the past few months, we've seen BTC and ETH reach historic highs almost every other week and shed up to 10% of their value within days. This means that if your entire portfolio is made of BTC, your wealth would be fluctuating up to 10% in a matter of days. Investors exposed to only BTC after the first boom of December 2017 had a significant portion of their portfolio impacted by the bear run that ensued in 2018.

However, if you were to add a few other cryptos to your portfolio, the volatility of single crypto would not impact your portfolio significantly.

As crypto has gained mainstream institutional traders have popularized many cryptos that traditional retail traders knew little about. Institutional traders conduct thorough fundamental analysis before putting their investment in a particular crypto, as we established earlier. This means that when diversifying your portfolio, you can follow in their footsteps. This has made it easier for retail traders to diversify their portfolio without doing back-breaking research of a particular crypto.

How to Diversify Your Crypto Portfolio?

There are several ways for you to diversify your crypto portfolio:

Diversifying through the type of crypto

With over 5000 cryptos available in the market, you have plenty to choose from. While it may take a lot of time to review all these cryptos, there are websites like CoinMarketCap which are dedicated to categorizing all the available cryptos by their market size, price, traded volume, volatility, and several coins in circulation. This certainly makes your research work easier.

However, you shouldn't just make random selections and invest a percentage of your portfolio. You might instead select given crypto based on their type. Here are some of the categories of cryptos:

- Transactional tokens, which are used as currencies like BTC

- Smart contract tokens: These allow the user to access the blockchain technology and develop DAPPs, allow decentralized payments, and run smart contracts on its platform. They include Ethereum, Binance Chain, and Polkadot.

- Yield-earning tokens: These allow users to earn interest by simply holding them in their crypto wallet.

- Utility tokens: these are tokens that allow the user to access certain specific services on an existing blockchain protocol

- Stablecoins: Tokens pegged to traditional currencies and assets, which can provide more stability and less volatility than traditional crypto tokens, like USDC and PAXGold. They are often used to hedge against the market.

Diversifying by Industry

This is akin to investing in stocks of companies that operate in different sectors of the economy. The idea behind this is that if one sector takes a hit, your portfolio is not exposed to it. There are several cryptos used in various industries. They include energy sector, finance, DeFi, data and analytics, identity, supply chain, AI, and medicine.

With this approach in mind, you may also choose to invest in crypto projects from various parts of the world.

Diversification by time

Time diversification involves investing in crypto over time. This covers the 'dollar cost averaging. Here's how. We have noticed that if you are to plot the price of cryptos, say BTC, you'll notice that it has been rising over time over time. This involves selecting the perfect timing to enter and exit the market. It is almost similar buy when low, selling when it high, and buying back again when prices fall. Another approach institution take is to buy cryptos consistently over, accumulating them. This means that they buy cryptos at different prices, which averages the price spent on the whole portfolio. This way, price volatility doesn't impact the value of the entire portfolio.

The primary goal of crypto investors is to diminish the costs involved in accumulating their portfolio. Diversifying crypto portfolios is one of the perfect ways of achieving this. These diversification tactics are not only viable for crypto investors but short terms traders as well.

Sophisticated crypto traders can take advantage of crypto derivatives.

Crypto Diversification Using Derivatives

In 2020, crypto derivatives gained popularity, especially with institutional investors who adopted options and futures to hedge against potential losses. Although crypto traders use derivatives to speculate on the future price movement of cryptocurrencies, crypto investors, especially institutional investors, adopt derivatives to hedge against a drop in the value of their portfolio.

Take the use of crypto options, for example.

They have put and call crypto options that are standardized and traded on crypto exchanges. A crypto option is a type of derivative that gives you the right to either buy or sell a specified amount of a particular crypto in the future for a specific price. This means that if an investor believes that their crypto value will drop in the future, they will use the crypto option to lock in a preferred price for their portfolio.

This contract will enable them to sell their portfolio at a specific price even if the future market price is significantly lower than the current price.

Similarly, investors can also use options contracts to accumulate their crypto portfolio at a cheaper price. If they speculate that the price of particular crypto will rise in the future, they use options contracts that allow them to lock in a specific price. This means that when the price of that crypto increases, the options contract allows them to accumulate their portfolio at a cheaper price even when the future market price is significantly higher. The best thing about options contracts is that the holder is not obligated to go through with that transaction.

5.6 Potential of Crypto Market & How Novice Traders Can Take Advantage?

Arguably, the crypto market blossomed in 2020 with the mainstream explosion of DeFi. This came along with several novel products and investment opportunities that are just beginning to unlock the potential of the crypto market. In the previous sessions, we have covered how crypto market participants can take advantage of. Here are some of the ways novice traders and investors can take advantage of the crypto market.

Trading with leverage

Leverage is also called margin. Leverage is a credit facility extended to you by your broker, which helps you increase your exposure to a particular asset. For example, if you take leverage of 100x, you will open a position that is 100x the size of your account deposit. Say you have a $1000 deposit in your account. With a leverage of 100x, you can open a position worth $100,000. Note that leverage can only be used when trading derivatives. It significantly increases your potential profits but also makes the downside huge. Traders use leverage in not only the spot market but also the futures market.

Staking

In December 2020, Ethereum rolled out Ethereum 2.0, which introduced staking. Proof of Staking is a consensus mechanism that is more efficient than the proof-of-work consensus, allowing users to earn passive income by staking their cryptos. Unlike the mining process for BTC, ETH is mined when users lock-in their cryptos to make them available to create new blocks. Since the staking process keeps the crypto network secure and eliminates the double-spending problem, users who stake their cryptos earn a reward.

The staking process involves:

- Selecting cryptos that use PoS consensus mechanism, such as ETH, and buy them

- Find a crypto software that allows staking, and store your cryptos in this wallet

- Determine the minimum number of particular crypto needed to stake. In ETH, for example, you have to stake a minimum of 32ETH and 10000 for XTZ. Note that some cryptos do not require a minimum staking amount; you stake any amount of crypto you have

- Select your preferred virtual private servers (VPS), which allows you to run everything in the cloud since the staking process requires that you have 24/7 uninterrupted internet access.

Crypto Lending

One of the greatest achievements of DeFi has been the advent of decentralized crypto lending using smart contracts. Smart contracts used in Ethereum refer to contracts that automatically execute when the terms agreed upon by the parties are attained. Unlike conventional contracts whose execution depends on counterparties and including a third party, the agreement terms in smart contracts are written within lines of codes. In this case, the contract executes itself, with the transaction being irreversible and transparent for all parties. Note that, as is with anything on a blockchain network, the smart contract is decentralized. The most notable achievement of

210

smart contracts is to enforce trust between anonymous parties eliminating the need for external enforcement mechanisms, legal systems, or central authority.

When crypto holders put their cryptos, the smart contracts pool together loans and codifies terms of the contract into the loans, which is then automatically distributed to lenders. This process is anonymous and efficient since there are no KYC or AML policies involved. The smart contract ensures that whoever is borrowing the cryptos has sufficient collateral and guarantees that crypto lenders won't lose their funds. Centralized crypto lending platforms operate like traditional banks.

By lending your cryptos, you can earn up to 0.1999% per day and compound your interest for as long as you'd want.

Dividend-paying Tokens

These are cryptos which help the holders earn dividend for simply storing them. It is one of the best ways to earn income passively. They are like holding shares in a public company – the coins have inherent value, but they also earn interest monthly, bi-annually or quarterly. The interest comes in the form of extra coin rewards for simply holding on to that crypto. Some of the best known interest-bearing cryptos are Stellar, Bankera and NEO.

Novice crypto traders and investors can also earn free coins that are received through airdrops and hard forks. New and sometimes existing projects use airdrops for marketing themselves. Hard forks happen when new crypto is created by deviating from existing crypto. One of the most prominent hard forks involved the creation of BCH from BTC. Here, the original holders of BTC received an equivalent amount of BCH.

The interest received from the dividend-paying tokens is rewarded for having faith in the brand. Novice traders and investors can diversify their portfolio with a variety of dividend-paying tokens.

Stablecoins

Stablecoins are cryptocurrencies whose value can be pegged on other assets. Mainstream cryptos such as Bitcoin and Ether tend to be highly volatile. This volatility makes cryptos popular to traders. However, for investors looking for a proper long-term store of value, the extreme volatility inherent in cryptocurrencies makes them unattractive.

Most investors – both institutional and individual – are increasingly seeking lesser volatile cryptocurrencies as a long-term store of value. This trend was precipitated by the unprecedented fiscal and monetary policies implemented by governments and central banks in 2020 to combat the coronavirus pandemic. However, these policies threatened the stability of fiat currencies by exposing them to inflation. With DeFi, auditing stablecoins becomes much easier, which ensures manageable volatility and adequate reserves. Stablecoins include:

- Cryptocurrency collateralized stablecoins. Their value is pegged on other cryptocurrencies. However, to mitigate the underlying volatility in cryptocurrencies, these coins are over-collateralized.

- Fiat collateralized stablecoins. Fiat currencies collateralize these coins in the ratio of 1 to 1.

- Non-collateralized stablecoins. The stability of these coins depends on an algorithm that determines the supply of the coins. The algorithm alters the supply based on demand. It is akin to the model most central banks use to control the economy's supply of physical cash.

Novice traders and investors can use stablecoins to hedge against the volatilities of cryptocurrencies and benefit from fiat. When such cryptos are held and used for lending, they offer the best way to protect one's portfolio while earning income passively. This means that investors can benefit when value appreciates and enjoy the interest paid from crypto lending.

Session 6
Technical Analysis

6.1 Introduction to Candlesticks

Charting the price action of a particular crypto can be done on a line chart, a bar, chart or using candlesticks. Candlesticks are by far the most popular among the price charting techniques. We dedicate this section to learning about what candlesticks are, how they look like, how they are formed, the various crypto candlestick patterns, and more importantly, the information conveyed by candlesticks.

Here's an example of a candlestick price chart.

Candlesticks are used to show the price information of a particular tradable asset over time. They were first used by Sokyu Honma, a Japanese rice trader in the late 17th century – hence the name 'Japanese

Candlesticks'. Since then, they have gained immeasurable popularity in financial trading due to their simplicity and accuracy. Here are some of the factors that led to the popularity of candlesticks:

- They are flexible and can be used on any timeframe, from a 5-second chart to yearly charts.

- They aggregate price data over the selected period. For example, if you select candlesticks on a 1-minute timeframe, that single candle stick will show you the opening price, the highest price attained during that minute, the lowest price, and the closing price.

- Candlesticks can also be used as technical analysis tools by their own. They show the general trend of an asset and its price momentum. Trader can opt to use candlestick analysis instead of crowding their crypto chart with several technical indicators

- Candlesticks can be used by any type of crypto trader, from a scalper, day trader, position trader, and swing traders. This is because, candlesticks can be plotted on any timeframe, and can be adjusted to show price information on various timeframes

- Candlesticks are color-coded green or red. Green candles show that the price is bullish while the red candles show that the price is bearish. This makes the process of analysis simple since bullish and bearish trends can be identified at a single glance.

- The candlestick patterns are also easy to comprehend

- Traders can use candlestick patterns to gauge the market's volatility

Anatomy of the Candlestick

A candlestick has a body and a wick (shadow). The body of the candlestick shows the opening and closing price. The upper wick shows the highest price during that timeframe while the lower wick shows the lowest price during that timeframe.

Basically, a single candlestick shows;

- The opening price
- The closing price
- The highest price

- The lowest price

Candlesticks can either be bullish or bearish. Typically, a bullish candlestick is green in colour. It forms when the opening price of an asset is lower than its closing price. Say for example you have a 1-minute bullish candlestick. It means that when that minute began, the opening price was lower than the price of that asset when 1-minute elapsed. It doesn't matter the volatility during that minute, regardless of the highest or the lowest price reached, provided the opening price is lower than the closing price, then that candle is a bullish candle.

Bullish Candlestick

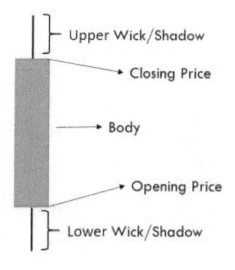

219

Conversely, a bearish candle is formed when the opening price is higher than the closing price. This means that the price dropped during that timeframe. For example, if you have a 1-minute bearish candle, it means that the during that minute, the price opened at a particular level, then closed lower after the one minute had elapse. Whether the price trended higher than the opening price or lower than the closing price, as long as the price closed lower than it opened, then it a bearish candle. Bearish candles are typically red in colour.

Bearish Candlestick

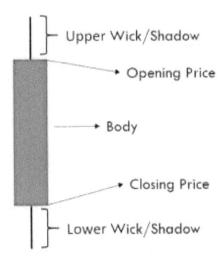

Note that you can change your chart settings and adjust the colour of bullish and bearish candles to your preference.

Different types of candlestick patterns
Owing to their diversity, analysts over the centuries have come up with several candlestick patterns. These candlestick patterns show direction and momentum of a price action, and can be categorized into single, dual and triple candlestick pattern depending on the number of candlesticks involved in determining a given pattern.

These candlestick patterns can also be used to identify continuation, reversal and trending crypto chart patterns. Continuation chart patterns mean that the observed market trend will continue in the observed direction. Reversal chart patterns mean that the current trend is about to change into an opposite trend, say a bullish trend reversing into a bearish trend, and vice versa. These patterns are also classified as bullish and bearish continuous and reversal pattern. Trending chart patterns mean that the market doesn't have a discernible trend – the price action is neither bullish nor bearish. We will discuss this further in Section 6.5

Single Candlestick patterns

These are candlestick patterns which are formed by the appearance of just one candlestick. In this case, a trading signal is generated by the appearance of the pattern formed by this one candlestick. Examples of single candlestick patterns are:

- Marubozu Candlestick Pattern
- Spinning Top Candlestick Pattern
- The Hanging Man Candlestick Pattern (the hammer)
- The Shooting Star Candlestick Pattern

Dual Candlestick Patterns

As the name suggest, these candlestick patterns are formed when two candlesticks appear together. These candlestick patterns can either be reversal or continuation candlestick patterns. They include:

- Engulfing Candlestick Pattern

- Tweezer Bottoms and Tops Candlestick Pattern
- Harami Candlestick Pattern
- Dark Cloud Cover Candlestick pattern

Triple Candlestick Patterns

The triple candlestick patterns form when three distinct candles appear in succession. They can form reversal or continuation price patterns. They include;

- Three White Soldiers Candlestick Pattern
- Falling Three Methods
- Morning Star Candlestick Pattern
- Three Inside Up Candlestick Pattern

6.2 Understanding Candlestick Patterns

We have covered some of the very well-known candlestick patterns in this part of the session. Please pay attention as understanding them can be a bit tricky.

The Marubozu Candlestick Pattern

The Marubozu pattern includes no upper and lower shadow. This candlestick pattern has just one candle with no wicks — it only has a body.

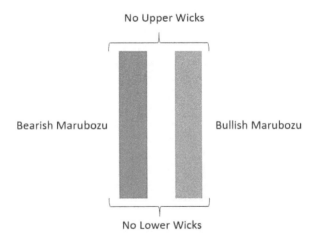

The Marubozu pattern can either be bullish and bearish, depending on the dominant trend in the market. In an uptrend, this pattern indicates that buyers are still dominant in the market and that the uptrend is likely to continue. The bullish Marubozu is green, meaning that the price increased steadily with no fluctuations or volatility during that period.

A bearish Marubozu pattern appears in a downtrend, implying that sellers are still dominant in the market. In this case, the bearish Marubozu has no wicks meaning that the price dropped steadily during that period with no volatility. This implies that the downtrend is likely to persist.

The image below shows the Marubozu candlestick pattern on a price chart

The Spinning Top Candlestick Pattern

Depending on the prevailing market trend, the spinning top candlestick pattern can indicate either a trend continuation of a trend reversal. A small candle body characterizes this pattern with long wicks. The upper and lower wicks are of the same size.

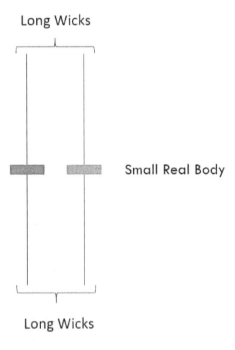

Long Wicks

Small Real Body

Long Wicks

This pattern means that neither the buyers nor the sellers dominated the market during that period. When this pattern appears, there are two possibilities;

- The market could potentially reverse in either direction, or
- There will be a continuation of the current trend

The price chart below represents how this pattern looks on a price chart

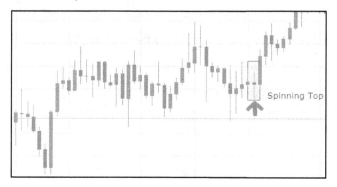

Spinning Top

When the spinning top candlestick pattern appears, it is recommended to use technical momentum indicators to identify the likelihood of the subsequent trend.

The Hanging Man Candlestick pattern

This pattern is a single pattern of the candlestick pattern that forms during an uptrend. It's a precursor to a looming downtrend. The pattern is characterized by a small candle body, no upper wick and a long lower wick.

It's a reversal pattern, which implies that the current trend is about to change into the opposite one. For example, it f appears in a bullish trend; it means that the trend is about to turn bearish. In this case, it shows that sellers are dominating the buyers in the market.

In a downtrend, the hanging man candlestick pattern's appearance shows that the market is about to turn bullish. This indicates that the short-selling pressure is getting exhausted, and buyers are about to push prices further higher.

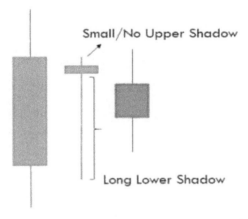

This is shown below in a picture of how this pattern will look at a price chart.

Pattern Confirmation Criteria:

- This is a single candlestick pattern that occurs after a small rally in the price. The rally of price can also be big, but it should be made of a few candles, which will move overall higher.

- The candle should have a small body and a lower wick at least two times the size of the body.

- This is only a warning, and a Bearish candle after the Pattern formation is highly wanted.

The appearance of this pattern can be used as a signal to exit a trade. If you have a long trade, you should exit your trade when the hanging man candlestick pattern forms since the pattern precedes a bearish trend.

Similarly, if you are short in the market, close your position when this pattern forms since it implies that the market is about to turn bullish.

The Shooting Star Candlestick Pattern

This candlestick pattern shows potential market reversal. A small body characterizes the single candlestick with a very short lower wick and a longer upper wick.

In an uptrend, this pattern forms when the momentum of the uptrend is waning. It forms near the lowest price in the trend. Typically, the shooting star candlestick pattern can be used as a resistance level. This means that, at this point, the buyers could not push an asset's price much higher since sellers flocked the market, pushing prices down.

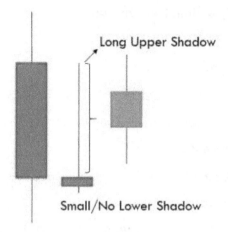

Long Upper Shadow

Small/No Lower Shadow

Below is a picture of how this pattern looks like on a price chart.

Shooting Star

Market Reversal

The uptrend

Pattern Confirmation Criteria

- This pattern should come after a sustained uptrend in the market.

- The distance between the highest and lowest price should be two times the length of the body of the candle.

- It's best if there will be no wick under the body of the candle.

Traders should not take action at once when this pattern is formed. They should wait and observe if a trend reversal begins to form. If a downtrend starts to form, they should confirm that a bearish trend will ensue.

Tweezer Tops and Bottoms Candlestick Pattern

This double candlestick pattern signifies trend continuation. The tweezer top is formed when the highs of two candlesticks occur at the same price level following a bullish candle. A bottoming pattern forms when the lows of two candles occur at the same price level, following a bearish trend.

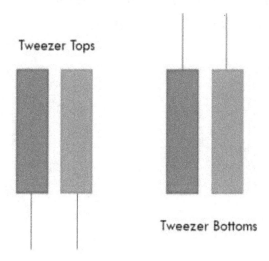

Tweezer Tops

Tweezer Bottoms

In this pattern, the first of the two candles show the direction of the short-term trend, while the second candle is seen as a pause to this trend, or possibly the start of its reversal. This shows that there has been a shift in the short-term momentum, suggesting that the price is likely to continue with the longer-term trend.

Here's how the tweezer tops and bottoms candlestick pattern look like on a price chart.

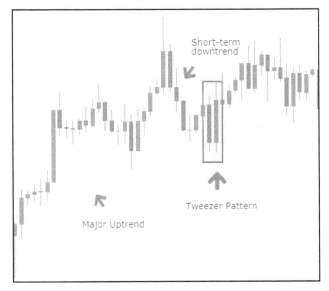

Pattern Confirmation Criteria

- The difference between the open and close should be large for the first candle, i.e., it should have a real body

- The size of the second candle can vary. However, if it is larger than the first candle, it means that the price can continue trending

Harami Candlestick Pattern

This is a dual candlestick pattern that indicates the continuation of a trend.

A bullish Harami shows that the short-term bearish trend is waning, and the market is likely to continue with the longer-term bullish trend. This pattern is characterized by a long candlestick followed by a relatively smaller body within the previous body's vertical range.

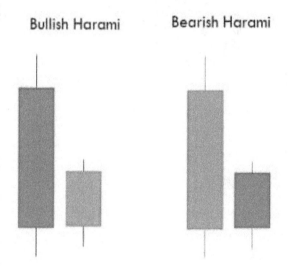

Bullish Harami   Bearish Harami

Below is a chart showing how a bullish Harami forms on a price chart. Notice that the preceding short-term trend is a bearish one; the small green candles show the short-term trend's reversal into an uptrend.

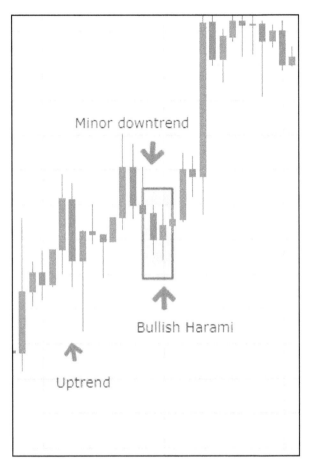

Pattern Confirmation Criteria

- In the short-term, there has to be a clear pattern that shows a bear market.

- The second candle in this pattern has to close near the middle of the previous candle. This shows that there is a higher likelihood that the price will reverse into an uptrend.

The Harami candlestick pattern should be used alongside single candlestick patterns to ensure the accuracy of the entry signals.

In this example, we have shown the bullish Harami. The bearish Harami forms in the exact opposite way.

Engulfing Candlestick Pattern

Engulfing is a two-candle trend reversal pattern, which derives its name from the fact that the second candle in the pattern completely overshadows the first candle.

A bullish engulfing candlestick pattern forms when a bearish candle (red) in a downtrend is preceded by a larger bullish candle (green), which completely engulfs it.

A bearish engulfing candlestick pattern forms when a green candle in an uptrend is followed by a large bearish candle that completely engulfs it.

Bullish Engulfing Pattern | Bearish Engulfing Pattern

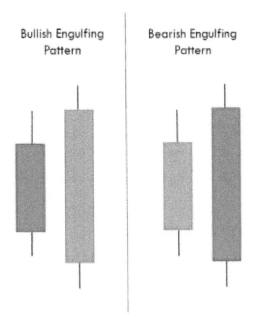

238

Here's an example of a bullish engulfing candlestick pattern on a price chart.

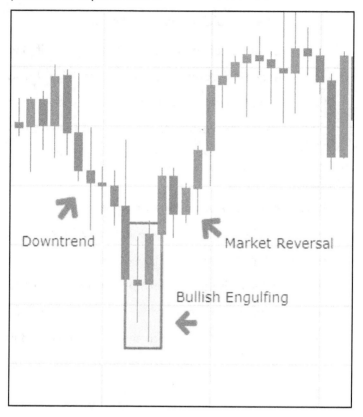

Criteria for the pattern:

- The body of the second candle should be considerably larger than the first candle in the pattern

- The best case for a reversal occurs if the engulfing candle is larger than at least three other candles preceding the pattern

- Chances of a reversal are higher if the engulfing candle has no upper wick for a bullish reversal and no lower wick for a bearish reversal. This implies that the price has been progressive with no volatility

Dark Cloud Cover Candlestick pattern

The Dark Cloud Cover pattern is a bearish reversal candlestick pattern formed by two candles.

Here, the bearish candle (red) opens above the first candle in the pattern and closes around the midpoint of the first candle. Note that the first candle in this pattern has to be a bullish candle towards the end of an uptrend.

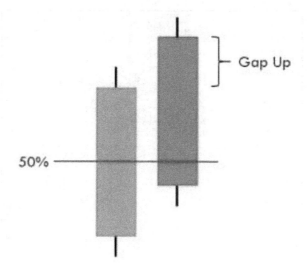

Gap Up

50%

The pattern shows buyers are struggling to push prices further higher, but sellers significantly gain control of the market, pushing prices down. When this momentum shifts, it causes the trend to reverse into bearish.

Here's how the Dark Cloud Cover pattern makes a reversal of the trend on a price chart.

Criteria for the pattern

- There must be a well-established uptrend on the price chart

- There should be a gap between the closing of the first candle and the opening of the second candle in the pattern

- The second candle should close at least around the midpoint of the first candle.

Typically, traders should wait for the confirmation of a trend reversal before making any short trades. The confirmation is often the formation of another bearish candle that closes below the second candles of the pattern.

Three White Soldiers Candlestick Pattern

This is a triple candlestick pattern and is classified as a continuation pattern. The appearance of the 'three white soldiers' candlestick pattern signifies the reversal of a short-term downtrend into a long terms bullish trend – this is why it's a continuation pattern.

The pattern is characterized by three long-bodied candles that open within the previous candle's body and close above the previous candle's high.

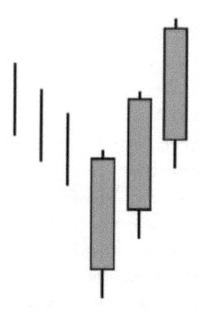

Here's how this pattern looks like on a price chart.

Criteria for the pattern

- The second and third candle sin the pattern must open within the body of the previous candle

- All the three candles in the pattern shouldn't have long wicks

- Often use momentum and technical directional indicators like the RSI and EMA to confirm the continuation of the trend.

Owing to its versatility, the Three White Soldiers pattern can be used to enter and exit a trade. For example, traders with short positions will exit the market when this pattern forms, and it can be used to open a long trade since a bullish trend follows it.

Falling Three Methods

The Falling Three Methods candlestick pattern is a trend continuation pattern. It's also known as the five-candle pattern since the candles confirm the existence of this trend form just before the three candles pattern begins and after the pattern ends.

Although it may look like a reversal, Falling Three Methods is a continuation pattern.

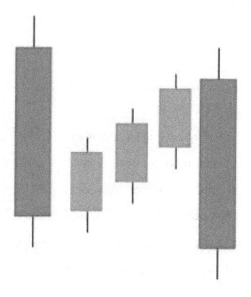

Here's how this pattern appears on a price chart.

Criteria for the pattern

- This candlestick pattern is a bearish continuation pattern with two long bearish candles on either side of the Falling Three Methods – which are bullish candles

- The series of small-bodied candles should be of the same colour. However, a bearish Doji as the third candle can also be considered.

Traders use this pattern to open new short positions or add on to existing short positions. Although this is a triple candlestick pattern, the fifth candle is the confirmation candlestick, indicating that the bearish trend will continue. Technical indicators can also be used to confirm entry positions.

Morning Star Candlestick Pattern

This is a three-candlestick pattern that signals the reversal of a trend. The pattern often occurs towards the end of a downtrend and signals a reversal into a bullish trend.

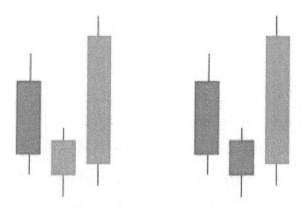

However, before buying into the market, traders often use a combination of technical momentum indicators to confirm that the downtrend is coming to an end. The RSI indicator is one of the most commonly used indicators since it shows when the market goes into the oversold territory. We have covered the RSI indicator in a later section.

Here's how the Morning Star Pattern looks like on a price chart

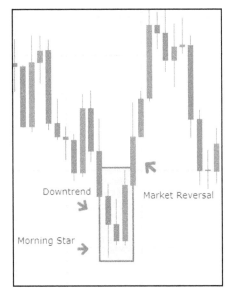

Criteria for the Morning Star pattern

- The first candle in this pattern is a long bearish candle with very small or no wicks

- The second candle in the pattern is often a small bearish or bullish candle. This signifies indecision in the market as buyers and sellers try to gain control of the market.

- The third candle in the pattern is a long bullish candle that confirms the reversal and marks a new uptrend.

Three Inside Up Candlestick Pattern

This is a three-candlestick pattern that indicates a reversal of a trend when they appear on a price chart. The pattern shows that the current trend is losing momentum, which could change into the opposite trend.

The Three Inside Up candlestick pattern is characterized by a bullish pattern composed of a large bearish candle, a smaller second candle that is overshadowed by the first candles, and a third bullish closes above the first candle.

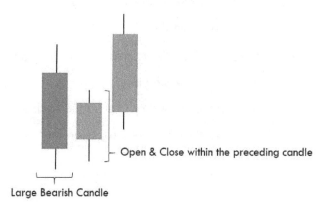

Open & Close within the preceding candle

Large Bearish Candle

Here's how this pattern appears on a price chart.

Criteria for the pattern

- The market should have a clear downtrend

- The first candle in the pattern should be a long bearish candle

- The second candle should open and close within the body of the first bearish candle. Note that the second candle should be bullish. This shows that buyers are returning to the market

- The third candle should be a long bullish candle that closes above the first candle of the pattern.

6.3 Learning to Read Crypto Price Charts

Learning to Read Crypto Price Charts

Reading crypto charts is an essential skill for any trader or investor in the crypto market. Without the knowledge of how to read crypto charts, any investment or trading attempts would be futile. This section will learn about the different crypto charts available, different timeframes that can be applied to the charts, and finally discuss different market trends and their phases.

Types of crypto price charts

In the crypto market, cryptos are often pairs. For example, ETH/BTC. This is a pair of Ethereum and bitcoin. The price chart of ETH/BTC shows the exchange rate between the two cryptos. Specifically, it shows the amount of BTC you would need to buy 1 ETH.

The crypto price chart for the pair plots the fluctuation in this exchange rate over time. You can plot this price fluctuation on a line chart, a bar chart or a candlestick chart.

ETH/BTC 'Bar' price chart

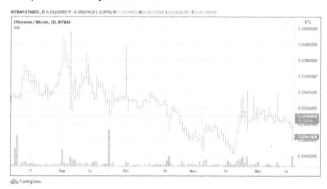

ETH/BTC 'Line' price chart

ETH/BTC 'Candlestick' price chart

These are the most popular crypto price charts, and you are guaranteed to find them on any trading platform. However, depending on the trading platform, several other crypto price charts including; hollow candles, Heikin Ashi, Area charts, Baseline charts, Renko charts, Line break charts, and Kagi Range charts, and Point & figure charts.

We recommend using candlestick charts since they are diverse and offer a lot of information regarding the crypto price. More so, candlestick price charts can also be used for technical analysis. We have discussed candlesticks in detail in the introductory section of this chapter. Later sections are dedicated to candlestick patterns and trends.

254

Timeframe for Crypto Price Charts

In trading, a timeframe refers to the grouping of price based on the amount of time it takes to form. Depending on the trading platform you use, timeframes can range from 1 second to 1 year.

A 1-second timeframe shows the price fluctuation during that second. It shows the opening price, the highest and lowest price attained, and the closing price for that period. The same applies to every other timeframe.

You can also view it this way; a 5-second price chart is a combination of five 1-second timeframes since it shows the price fluctuation for 5 seconds. Similarly, a 1-hour timeframe is a combination of 60 1-minute timeframes. In this case, the opening price of the 1-hour timeframe is the same as the opening price for the first 1-minute candle. Similarly, the closing price for the 1-hour timeframe is equal to the closing price of the 60th 1-minute candle.

You can use this logic to break down any timeframe into smaller timeframes or build a larger timeframe from a series of smaller timeframes.

Using Timeframes in Price Analysis

Traders often use the different timeframes available for price chart analysis. This is called multiple timeframe analysis.

For example, like a crypto scalper, a short-term trader will use a series of shorter-period timeframes to analyse price fluctuation in the short-term and identify the general trend. This is a top-down timeframe analysis technique that involves analysing the larger timeframe followed by subsequent timeframes. This technique helps break down the timeframes and determine how the subsequent trends divert from the observed general trend.

For example, if a crypto scalper wants to buy, they switch their chart to a 30-minute timeframe and observe the general trend. If they observe a general bullish trend, they will break down the chart to a 15-minute timeframe to confirm if the same bullish trend still holds. They would switch to 5-minute timeframe to identify the optimal Point to open a position if it does.

This top-down timeframe analysis technique is applied by all other traders in the crypto market. However, the timeframes used vary depending on their intended trading duration. The table below shows different timeframes for a different type of traders.

Category	Type of Trader	Trend	Trigger Timeframe
Long term	Position trader	Weekly	Daily
Medium-term	Swing trader	8-hour to Daily	4-hour
Short term	Day trader	4-hour to 8-hour	Hourly
	Scalper	Hourly	5-minute

We have covered these types of traders in detail in section 6.3.

Different Market Trends and their Phases

Market trends describe the general direction of the price fluctuation. There are three phases of a market trend that can be identified form reading the crypto price charts. Typically, the price of crypto doesn't move in a single direction. For a period, the price could be moving in a downtrend, then reverses to an uptrend, and there are times when the price has no

258

specific trend. It is neither in an uptrend nor a downtrend. All this information can be seen on a price chart just by a single glance.

A Bearish Crypto Price Chart

A downtrend on a price chart shows that the price of the crypto is falling. Remember that cryptos are often in pairs, like ETH/BTC. When you notice a downtrend, it means that either the value of ETH is dropping relative to BTC or that the value of BTC is increasing relative to ETH.

In a bearish trend, all the candles don't need to be bearish, there are instances where bullish candles will appear, but the general trend remains bearish.

Here's how the downtrend looks like on a crypto price chart.

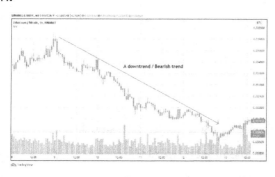

A Bullish Crypto Price Chart

A bullish crypto price chart represents a period when the price of crypto is increasing. Using the example of the ETH/BTC pair, a bullish trend implies that the value of ETH is increasing at a faster rate compared to that of BTC. It could also mean that the value of BTC is dropping compared to that of ETH.

In a bullish trend, all the candles formed don't necessarily need to be bullish. There might be a few instances where bearish candles appear, but the general trend remains bullish.

Here's how a bullish trend looks like.

A non-trending Crypto Price Chart

As we mentioned earlier, a crypto price doesn't necessarily need to be either on a bullish or bearish trend. Sometime, the market could be in a non-trending pattern where the price seems to be trading within a horizontal channel. In this case, the price chart is neither bullish nor bearish. Most of the time, this happens when the market sentiment is neutral.

Typically, this type of trend often occurs when the market is transitioning from a bullish to bearish trend or bearish to a bullish trend. Here's an example.

6.4 Different Trading Techniques

The crypto trading market has grown astronomically over the past few years and has attracted traders from all walks of life. These traders have different trading techniques best suited to their trading goals, market outlook, and amount invested. Different trading techniques can be categorized into four distinct techniques – intraday trading, swing trading, position trading, and scalping. Before we dive into the different trading techniques, let's first revisit the difference between trading and investing.

Trading involves buying or selling cryptocurrencies over the short term – i.e., going long or short. Trading focusses on maximizing short-term gains by taking advantage of volatility and media hype. Traders often spend most of their time observing chart patterns and analyzing trends before deciding whether to go short or long.

Most traders also use proprietary tools and techniques to enhance their profits. They also take advantage of the various order types to help them open and close positions under specific market conditions. Risk management techniques such as the use of leverage and stop-loss levels are also handy to traders.

In a nutshell, traders aim to profit in the market by taking advantage of short-term volatility. Primarily, most traders use leverage to increase the size of their positions and magnify their potential profits. More so, traders often prefer to trade contract for difference (CFD) assets than own the underlying assets.

Investing involves buying and holding an asset over the longer term. Investing is focused on the bigger picture, and investors tend to ignore the shorter-term price fluctuation and concentrate on the fundamental quality of the asset.

The primary goal of investors is to attain the maximum possible return on investment by holding as an asset for the maximum duration possible. In investing, it is believed that in the long run, the asset will appreciate; that is why investors will overlook the short-term price volatility and even continue accumulating their portfolio size when the price is low.

Note that investing involves buying and owning the actual asset. For example, a Bitcoin investor will buy and receive BTC in their wallet. This means that there is no leverage involved when investing. One of the most significant advantages of investing is that if the market crashes, you will only lose the equivalent of the amount you have invested. However, this is rarely the case since it is unheard of for the price of an asset to drop to $0. Compared to trading, a small market shift in the opposite direction could wipe out a trader's capital and sometimes run a negative balance when using leverage.

Let's now try to understand different popular crypto trading techniques.

Scalping trading technique

Scalpers are traders who open and close positions within a very short period. The duration of a single trade could range from a few seconds to a couple of minutes. Scalpers do not remain in a position for long as their primary goal is to earn as many pips in a very short period. Market volatility is a scalper's best friend. With frequent market volatility, scalpers can open a long position, close it if a few minutes, open a short position... and so forth.

In a single trade, scalpers often target 3 to 4 pips, which over the long run, accumulate massive profits. In crypto trading, the growth of derivatives and CFDs has made scalping popular among crypto traders. Successful scalping often requires precise technical analysis and chart analysis skills. This way, scalpers can easily and almost effortlessly identify accurate trading opportunities. Scalping often relies on minute charts to identify trading opportunities.

Intraday Trading

As the name suggests, intraday trading involves opening and closing positions within the trading day — no position remains open overnight. Day traders do not necessarily keep their positions open throughout the day. Some of the positions can only remain open for a few hours. That is because intraday traders often have a minimum target number of pips they aim to earn in a day. When this goal is achieved, they close their positions and call it a day. However, if they won't have achieved their daily trading objective by the end of the day, they also close any open positions.

Typically, intraday traders also rely heavily on technical analysis when executing their trades. Observing the short-term and medium price action helps them identify the ideal entry and exit positions. Intraday traders rely on hourly and daily charts to set up their trades.

Swing trading

Unlike scalpers and day traders, swing traders often seek to accumulate larger profits by keeping their positions open for longer periods, typically ranging from a few weeks to months. Swing traders aim to take advantage of the subsequent news release. By definition, swing trading involves buying and selling cryptos after significant price fluctuations.

Crypto swing traders incorporate both sentimental and technical analyses to inform their trade decisions. Swing traders can either go long or short. When they go short, they enter into a position when the market sentiment is at its highest and is bound to wane. Since cryptos are demand-driven, their price tends to be susceptible to public sentiment. Conversely, when swing traders go long, they enter when the public sentiment is beginning to rise.

Note that swing trading involves a painstaking amount of market analysis and monitoring trades. This makes it highly unpopular to novice traders. Effective swing trading involves a four-point plan:

- Ensure you have a clear plan of when the market conditions are ideal for you to enter and exit a position
- Invest what you can afford to lose. This might seem like a no-brainer, but it is crucial. Swing traders must have thick skin and have the mental fortitude to ride out short term fluctuations. If you invest a significant portion of your portfolio in swing trading, you might be tempted to exit your trade prematurely
- Use stop-loss and trailing stop to limit your downside in case of extreme volatility. Remember that cryptocurrencies are inherently volatile and that no matter how proficient you are in market

analysis, there are always chances of a loss. Using SL and trailing stop, keep the uncertainties under control.

- Watch out for Bitcoin. When it comes to cryptos, Bitcoin is king! The fluctuation in most cryptos always tends to follow BTC's fluctuations. So, being aware of Bitcoin's activity will help you make more informed decisions.

Position trading

Position traders hold their positions for very long periods, averaging a couple of months. In most cases, it is considered an extended version of swing trading. This trading technique shares fundamental properties with crypto HODLing since they buy cryptos and hold on to them for a longer period.

However, position traders may cash out their portfolios along the way if the market starts to trend against them. They also open new positions along the way when prices dip. This trading technique is one of the simplest, but it requires patience, self-discipline and a good understanding of sentimental analysis.

Position traders need to conduct thorough due diligence to establish the viability and sustainability of the project before investing. That is because they will be holding that particular crypto for the long-term, and no one wants to hold on to a dud!

6.5 Comprehending Crypto Price Patterns

What are Crypto Chart Patterns?

For crypto traders, chart pattern analysis is an invaluable part of trading. Crypto chart patterns are the trends that the price of a cryptocurrency forms over time, as the price fluctuates. These chart patterns often show a particular trend in price action and form the basis of technical analysis. Crypto chart patterns are categorized into two primary categories – trending crypto chart patterns and reversal crypto chart patterns. In this article, we will break down the top 10 crypto chart patterns that you will find useful in the course of trading.

Trending Crypto Chart Patterns

These are chart patterns that indicate the price of particular crypto will continue trading in the prevailing trend. They are also called continuation patterns. In many instances, trending chart patterns form when the price action consolidates but instead of a reversal, the price continues trading in the previously observed trend. Below are some of the most notable crypto trending chart patterns.

Cup & Handle Crypto Chart Pattern

The cup and handle crypto chart pattern signals a bullish continuation in price action. As the name suggests, this pattern occurs when the price action consolidates from a bullish trend forming a U-shaped "depression" that resembles a cup and a downward price movement that looks like a cup's handle.

The cup often forms after a sustained uptrend. It represents the period where the crypto price is pulling back after the sustained uptrend. This pullback doesn't wipe out the gains from the uptrend. This pullback will be followed by an equivalent price rally resulting in the U-shape. After the rally, the price will then trade in a sideways channel forming the "handle". Typically, after the handle is formed, the market experiences a renewed rally with the price breaking above the previous highs formed by the 'cup'. This breakout results in the continuation of the previous uptrend.

Note that depending on the timeframe you are trading, it may take a while for the cup and handle crypto chart pattern to form fully.

The Triangle Crypto Patterns

The triangle crypto chart patterns can be ascending, descending, or symmetrical.

Ascending triangle pattern: is a bullish continuation pattern. The high price swings form a horizontal line in this pattern, while the lower price swings form a rising trendline – these two lines form a triangle.

You can identify the ascending triangle chart pattern under these conditions:

- The market is in an uptrend which is followed by price consolidation
- The price forms higher lows and a rising trendline can be drawn connecting the higher lows. This shows that short sellers are getting exhausted and cannot push the price much lower since buyers are pushing price higher
- High price swings do not go beyond the flat upper trendline, which is the resistance level.
- The price breaks through the upper trendline, which is confirmation of the trend continuation.

273

When trading the ascending triangle pattern, entry points form when the price breaks out above the upper horizontal line.

Descending triangle pattern: is the opposite of the ascending triangle pattern. The descending chart pattern shows a bearish price continuation. These are the conditions necessary for the formation of a descending triangle.

- The market is in a sustained downtrend, followed by a short price rally.
- The price forms lower highs and a dropping trendline can be drawn connecting the lower highs. This shows buyers are getting exhausted in the market and that short sellers are pushing the price further downwards.
- Lower price swings do not trade below a flat horizontal trendline. Connecting the downward sloping trendline and the flat bottom line forms a descending triangle.
- A bearish continuation forms when the price breaks below the flat horizontal bottom line.

Symmetrical triangle chart pattern: show price consolidation. This pattern is characterized by the market forming higher lows and lower highs simultaneously. When you draw a trendline connecting the lower highs and another connecting the higher lows, they appear to be converging. This chart pattern is also called a pennant.

Note that the symmetrical triangle pattern can be either a continuation or a reversal chart pattern. Continuation occurs when the price breaks out in the direction similar to the price action before consolidation. The reversal occurs if the price breakout is opposite to that before consolidation.

Rectangle Crypto Chart Pattern

The rectangle chart pattern is the simplest and most popular among the top 10 crypto chart patterns since it easily identifies both continuation and trend reversals. However, traders prominently use the rectangle pattern to show trend continuation, since the prior trend's momentum provides an added advantage.

The pattern is formed during price consolidation after a sustained bullish or bearish trend. During the consolidation, the crypto asset trades in between two horizontal channels of support and resistance. This means that when you draw a horizontal line touching the price highs and another touching the price lows during the consolidation, they form a rectangular pattern.

Flag Crypto Patterns

The flag pattern is a continuation chart pattern which forms after a short period of consolidation following a persistent trend in one direction. This chart pattern can either be bullish or bearish flag pattern.

There has to be a prior uptrend for the bullish flag pattern, which forms the "pole" of the flag pattern — followed by a short price pullback period. When you draw trend lines on the consolidation, they form a downward pointing flag.

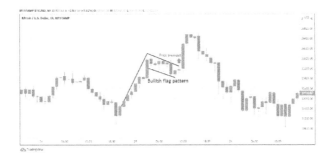

A bearish flag pattern forms after a short upward price consolidation following a sharp downtrend. Here, the bearish flag points upwards and has a positive slope.

In the bullish flag chart pattern, price continuation occurs after the price breaks out above the resistance level. For the bearish flag, the bear trend continues when the price breaks out below the support level.

Reversal Crypto Chart Patterns

Reversal crypto chart patterns mark a period where the prevailing market trend shifts into an opposite trend. For example, if the prevailing trend was bullish, a reversal chart pattern indicates that the market is about to adopt a bearish trend. In this case, it shows that sellers are exerting downward pressure in the market. Similarly, if the prevailing is bearish, a reversal chart pattern forms when the market is shifting into an uptrend.

Here's a brief description of the top reversal crypto chart patterns.

Head and Shoulders Crypto Pattern

The head and shoulders chart pattern represents trend reversal from bullish to bearish. Typically, this pattern forms after a bullish trend. It is characterized by price swings which form three peaks – the left shoulder, the head, and the right shoulder.

The left shoulder forms when there is a price pullback. After this pullback, the price will swing back up, to a level higher than the prior high. However, this price rally won't be sustained as sellers will push it downwards to the level of the previous swing low. The right shoulder is formed after buyers attempt to push the price back up, but fail to reach the previously attained levels (the head). Short sellers push the price downwards. This is a confirmation that bears are dominating the market.

When you draw a trendline from the lows of the first shoulder and the second shoulder, you'll notice that they are approximately on the same level. This is the "neckline", and it forms the support level. If the price breaks below it, it's an indicator that a bear trend is beginning.

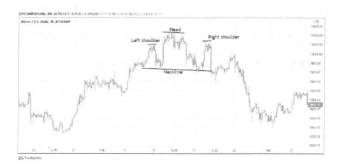

If you intend to trade a reversal using the head and shoulder crypto chart pattern, you must wait until the entire chart pattern forms.

Double/Triple Tops and Bottoms Chart Pattern

Double tops pattern signals reversal of a bullish trend to a bearish trend. This chart pattern occurs when the price forms two peaks at the same level. These peaks represent the resistance level reached by the asset during a bullish trend.

During an uptrend, the price reaches the first peak then pulls back slightly to a support level. The price then bounces back to a second peak touching the resistance level created by the first peak. This pattern shows that buyers cannot push the price beyond the resistance level and that the bullish momentum is dissipating. Consequently, the prices drop below the support level and adopt a bearish trend.

Triple tops are similar to double tops only that they form three instead of two peaks. The triple tops chart pattern is a bearish reversal pattern. The three peaks formed are approximately at the same support level. This implies that the support level is tested at least three times before the price adopts a bearish trend.

A double bottoms chart pattern is a bullish reversal pattern and considered the opposite of the double bottoms chart pattern. When the price is on a steady downtrend, it reaches a level where sellers cannot push the prices much lower. This is where the first bottom is formed – a resistance level where prices cannot go much lower. The price retraces to a higher support level, but the short-sellers push the price back down, forming a second bottom at the resistance level. Buyers overwhelm the sellers in the market, causing the prices to bounce off the resistance level reversing the downtrend.

A **triple bottoms** chart pattern is the opposite of the triple tops chart pattern. The pattern is formed like the double bottoms chart pattern but has three swing lows at approximately the same level. The prior bearish trend is reversed when the price breaks above the resistance level.

Rounded Tops and Bottoms Crypto Chart Pattern

Typically, the rounded tops and bottoms crypto chart pattern is used to identify longer-term reversal trends. Since it forms over a longer period, this pattern represents a gradual reversal of a trend.

Traders use a rounded tops chart pattern to identify long-term bearish reversal pattern. It signals the ending of a bullish trend and the start of a possible bear trend. This chart pattern resembles an inverted U. It occurs when, after a long-term bull run, the price consolidates for an extended period forming a rounded top. Subsequently, the price drops below the 'neckline' signalling the start of a downtrend.

Conversely, the rounded bottom chart pattern is a bullish reversal pattern showing the end of a bear run and a possible beginning of a bullish trend. In this case, the asset price has to consolidate for a long period, after a sustained downtrend, forming a U-shaped pattern. Eventually, the price will start rising and break above the 'neckline' signalling the start of a bull run.

The Failure Swing Trading Crypto Chart Pattern

This chart pattern often occurs when large speculative traders fail to form new highs or lows. These speculators often enter positions by taking advantage of deferred liquidity accumulated by other traders through limit orders such as buy and sell stop and stop-loss levels.

These large speculators attempt a swing trade by placing large orders in a relatively narrow price range.

In a bear market, failure swing trading occurs when short-sellers unsuccessfully attempt to achieve new lows. This is often a signal of an impending reversal of the downtrend into an uptrend. The bear trend reversal is completed when the price breaks through a prior high.

Similarly, the pattern in the bull market forms after buyers attempt and fail to form new highs. The bull trend reversal is completed when the price breaks through the previous low and adopts a downtrend.

Chart analysis is the backbone of technical analysis in crypto trading, and we have covered the top 10 crypto chart patterns that you will find helpful when trading. Most of the chart patterns we have discussed can be used for price action analysis across any timeframe. However, although most crypto traders use these chart pattern analyses to support their trades, we strongly recommend that you conduct thorough backtests when selecting which crypto chart pattern analysis best suits your trading style.

287

Moreover, since the crypto market tends to be relatively volatile, you should use these chart pattern analyses alongside other technical indicators. This will help improve the accuracy of your entry and exit levels.

6.6 Reliable Crypto Trading Strategies

A trading strategy is a technique that crypto traders use to enter and exit positions. These strategies determine if a trader should go long or short, and at what point to close that particular trade. Typically, crypto trading strategies are based on technical and sentimental analysis.

Technical analysis involves using technical indicators – often inbuilt on the trading platform to determine trend and momentum of a particular crypto. It also involves analysing crypto chart patterns to establish to establish general trend and determine the support and resistance levels. Sentimental analysis involves analysis of the prevailing public's opinion regarding a specified crypto.

In this session, we will cover the most reliable crypto trading strategies – based on technical indicators, and then late cover the top crypto trading chart patterns.

The Stochastic Oscillator Trading Strategy

For every trader, price action analysis is one of the primary factors that go into making a trade decision. The stochastic oscillator is a momentum indicator. It shows when the asset is at the overbought or the oversold territory by comparing the price changes over a specified period. It helps decide when to enter and exit a position at the most optimal price points. The stochastic oscillator helps crypto traders to do just that.

Remember, in the crypto market, the forces of demand and supply majorly determine the price of a currency pair. Therefore, when there are net buyers, the price is bound to go up, and when there are net sellers, the price can be expected to drop. The stochastic oscillator is the perfect indicator to use as a pressure gauge between buyers and sellers.

Components of the Stochastic Oscillator

The stochastic oscillator is a range-bound indicator; which means it has an upper bound of 100 and a lower bound of 0. Traders can adjust these bounds depending on their trading style. For this analysis, we will use the upper bound as 80 and the lower bound as 20.

The indicator itself is made up of two lines. A %k line also called the fast-stochastic line, and a %D line also called the slow stochastic line. The crossover between these two lines is used to generate buy or sell signals.

Identifying Overbought Regions with the Stochastic Oscillator

The stochastic oscillator compares the closing prices of a currency pair with the highest and lowest prices recorded during the selected period. It then ranks the closing price from the range of 0 to 100.

When the price of an asset goes beyond the upper bound, it means that the asset is overbought. This is a result of persistent buying pressure in the market, which results in the price going higher. Often, when the price reaches the overbought region, it is an indicator that the asset is recording higher highs.

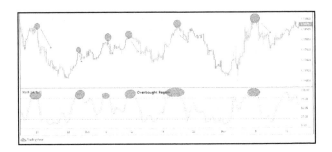

When an asset is oversold, it means that the buying pressure is about to dissipate since traders who are in long positions will start taking profits. Therefore, the buyers in the market will turn into sellers which in turn creates downward pressure on the price. We can expect that when the price reaches the overbought region, a short-selling signal is generated since the price will drop.

Identifying Oversold Regions with the Stochastic Oscillator

An asset enters the oversold region when the stochastic oscillator crosses below the lower bound of 20. This implies that there is a persistent pressure in the market by the short sellers driving the prices down. Most of the time, when the asset reaches the oversold territory, it implies that the pressure from the sellers has forced it to record lower lows.

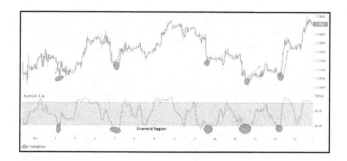

At the oversold region, the sellers in the market are exhausted. Their selling momentum is dissipating as they embark on profit-taking. We can, therefore expect that there will be a trend reversal since the sellers in the market are turning to buyers. When there are net buyers, the price will be pressured upwards. The price reaching the oversold region is an indicator of an imminent reversal of the downtrend into an uptrend.

Identifying Buy Signal using Stochastic crossover

A stochastic crossover occurs when the fast-moving stochastic line intersects with the slow-moving stochastic line.

A buy signal is generated when the fast-moving stochastic line (%k line) crosses the slow-moving stochastic line (%D line) from below and rises above it. When this happens, it means that there is a buying pressure in the market. This causes the market price to move in an uptrend faster.

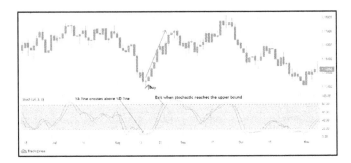

Only open a long position when the immediate candle after the %k to cross above the %D line is bullish. This is a confirmation that the upward pressure by the buyers is gaining momentum. It also helps you to avoid any fake-out crossovers.

Note that the best point to exit a long trade after a crossover is when the stochastic line reaches the upper bound. At this region, you can expect the price to enter into the overbought territory where the upward momentum reduces.

Identifying a Sell Signal using Stochastic crossover

A sell signal is generated when the %k line crosses below the %D line. This shows that sellers in the market are exerting a downward pressure resulting in a faster drop in the price leading to a sustained downtrend.

Only initiate a short position when the immediate candle after the %k crosses below %D line is a bearish candle. It confirms that the downward pressure by the net sellers is gaining momentum.

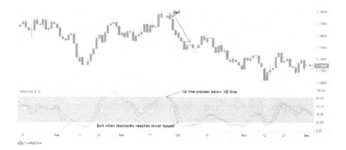

Make sure to exit the short position when the stochastic reaches the lower bound. It is expected that the downtrend momentum will slow when the price enters the oversold territory.

Note that sometimes the stochastic oscillator is prone to generating false crossover signals. A crossover might occur but fail to follow through. In such cases, it is highly recommended to use the stochastic oscillator with another technical indicator to confirm your entry points.

Identifying Divergence using the Stochastic Oscillator

Divergence happens when the stochastic oscillator does not reflect the highs and lows reached by the price of a crypto pair.

A bearish divergence occurs when the price of a currency pair reaches new higher highs, but the stochastic oscillator does not register corresponding new highs. Remember that the stochastic oscillator is a momentum indicator. Therefore, when it fails to register new higher highs along with the price action, it means that the momentum of the uptrend is getting weaker. Thus, we can expect a trend reversal.

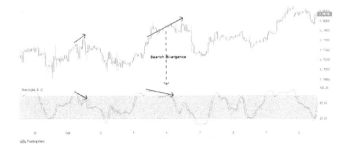

A bullish divergence occurs when the price action is registering new lower lows while the stochastic is registering new higher lows. This trend shows that the momentum of the downtrend is beginning to slow down and we can expect a reversal for an uptrend.

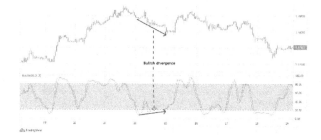

If you intend to trade stochastic Divergence, it is recommended to use other technical indicators to confirm entry positions. The reason for this is because the price may continue in the current trend before a reversal.

In other instances, you might observe that there is selling pressure on the stochastic oscillator, but the price action doesn't show the same momentum. This implies that the buyers are absorbing the selling pressure in the market, and it is more likely that the price action will move in an uptrend. Here's an illustration.

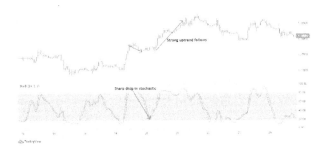

Similarly, you may observe that the stochastic oscillator shows a sharp momentum uptrend, but there is minimal uptrend registered by the price action. This shows that sellers are toning down the uptrend pressure exerted by the buyers in the market. Consequently, we can expect the price to have a breakout downtrend. Here's an example.

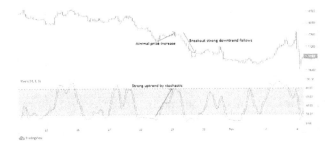

Although the stochastic oscillator is a reliable technical indicator, we recommend that you use it alongside other indicators. The reason behind this is because the stochastic oscillator was primarily designed to measure the momentum of the price change and not the trend.

Pros

- Provides several trading signals

- It's one of the simplest and dynamic trading strategies and can identify both trend and momentum.

Cons

- The major problem with Stochastic is sometimes, in a trending market gives a lot of false signal.

- Price divergence shown by this strategy may be reliable, but it is difficult to determine when the trend reversal will occur.

RSI Scalping Strategies

In crypto trading, scalping is a trading strategy where crypto traders open and close positions within short periods. The primary goal of this strategy is to gain as many pips in the shortest possible time. For crypto scalpers, the best trading time is when there is increased volatility in the market. To this end, the Relative Strength Index (RSI) indicator is a scalper's best friend. In this guide, we'll discuss the best strategies that a crypto scalper can implement when trading.

What is RSI?

The Relative Strength Index is a technical indicator which shows the strength and momentum of the price of a currency pair. The indicator consists of a line graph which oscillates between the 0 and 100 level. Here's how it works. When the RSI line is above 70, the asset is considered to be overbought, and when below 30, it's considered oversold. Using these two levels, a crypto trader can predict reversal points.

The RSI can also form chart trends and patterns which the price chart fails to show such as double tops, double bottoms and trends. With these, crypto scalpers can use the RSI indicator to identify the beginning of market trends and when these trends come to an end.

Scalping with RSI Divergence

For a crypto scalper, following the trend can help prevent premature exits. This will enable you to collect as many pips as possible. The RSI divergence occurs when the price chart forms a higher high, and the RSI forms a lower high. Similarly, the price charts could be forming lower lows while the RSI is forming higher lows. Both these scenarios can be used as a short term signal of a trend reversal. Here's an example set-up. For a crypto scalper, an uptrend can be spotted when the RSI is forming higher lows. Set the RSI Indicator period to 5 and use the 1-minute timeframe.

When the RSI forms the first higher low just above 30, open a long position. A series of higher lows is an indicator that the price is on an uptrend. You can open a long trade when the first higher low forms above 30. Exit the trade when the RSI forms a higher low just above 70.

The RSI can be used to trade in a downtrend when the RSI indicator is forming a succession of lower highs. For the downtrend, open a short trade can be

301

initiated when the first lower high is formed. This trade can be closed when a lower high is formed just around 30.

With this strategy, the average number of pips that can be earned is 5 pips. So, always set your 'stop loss' and 'take profit' levels at 5 pips.

Scalping Breakouts with RSI

A breakout occurs when the RSI line crosses either above 70 or below 30. To properly execute the scalping breakout strategy, make sure always to check the prevailing trend on the longer timeframes. The reason for this is that the trends in longer timeframes are made up of shorter timeframe trends. To trade breakouts, set the RSI indicator period to 2.

To trade a bullish breakout, open a position when the RSI line crosses 70. Close the trade when the line reaches the 100 level. Before scalping the bullish breakout on a 1-minute chart with the RSI, ensure that the 5-minute price chart shows an uptrend.

To trade a bearish breakout, open a short position when the RSI crosses below30. Close the position when the RSI indicator reaches the 0. Before scalping the bearish breakout on a 1-minute chart with the RSI, ensure that the 5-minute price chart is on a downtrend.

When scalping breakouts using the RSI indicator, the average number of pips expected is 6. Remember to set your 'stop loss' and 'take profit' levels at 5 pips.

Scalping with the RSI Indicator and Bollinger Bands Combination

With the combination of the Bollinger Bands and the RSI, we can spot the entry and exit positions more precisely. For this combination, set the period for the Bollinger Bands at 14 with a standard deviation of 2.0

Set the RSI indicator to a period of 5.

The Bollinger Bands can be used to show market trends which will aid in filtering out some impulsive movements of the RSI.

When the price touches the upper band, it means that the asset is overpriced. The signal to short sell arises when the RSI indicator is crossing 70 from the overbought region while the price is bouncing off the upper Bollinger Band. That means that the traders are taking profits, and sellers are prevalent in the market; thus, the price is bound to fall.

The exit signal for this trade is when the price reaches the lower Bollinger Band and the RSI entering the oversold region below 30. That shows the asset is cheap, and short sellers will be taking their profits; thus, the price is bound to start rising.

The signal to go long is generated when the price is bouncing off the lower Bollinger Band while the RSI indicator is crossing above 30. It means that the short sellers are taking profit, and buyers will be dominant in the market since the price is low. Thus, the price will rise.

The exit signal for the long trade occurs when the price touches the upper Bollinger Band as the RSI indicator enters the overbought region above 70.

Note when scalping using a combination of Bollinger Bands and the RSI indicator, the average number of pips for this combination is 7. So, set your 'stop loss' and 'take profit' levels at 7 pips.

To successfully scalp with the RSI indicator, you need to have discipline and adhere to the above strategies. Always wait for the precise moment when the RSI gives you the entry signal to open a position and avoid jumping in too early or getting in on the trend too late. Remember, you can always adjust the parameters of the RSI indicator and find optimal levels that might suit you.

Moving Average Convergence Divergence (MACD) Indicator

Moving average convergence divergence (MACD) is a technical indicator that shows the trend and momentum of an asset's price. It is used to determine the current price trend, its strength and the probability of a reversal. For a trader, the MACD is especially useful to support one's price action analysis, especially when it comes to identifying entry and exit points for a trade. The main usefulness of the MACD indicator is showing when the momentum of a trend is strong, and when it is weakening.

In this article, we will show you the components of the MACD indicator and also help you understand how you can use it to support your price analysis.

Components of the MACD Indicator

The MACD indicator has four components – the MACD line, a signal line, a histogram, and a 0-line which the MACD line and the signal line oscillate around.

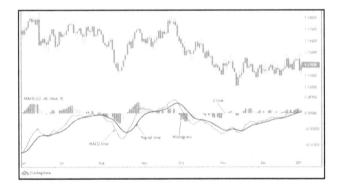

The MACD Line

The MACD line is derived from subtracting the 26-period EMA from the 12-period EMA. Here is a general formula for calculating the EMA. The 12-period EMA is called the fast EMA, and the 26-period is the slow EMA.

To calculate the MACD line, you have to calculate the fast EMA then subtract the slow EMA from it.

MACD line = 12-period EMA – 26-period EMA

Signal line

The signal line is the equivalent of the 9-period EMA. You can use the above EMA formula to determine this.

The zero line

Remember, the MACD oscillates between 1 and -1. The zero lines sit between these two extreme values. The zero lines are useful when it comes to determining whether the asset price is bullish or bearish, as we will see later.

MACD histogram

The MACD histogram is the difference between the MACD line and the signal line.

Histogram = MACD line – Signal line

By design, it is meant to be a predictor of an impending crossover between the MACD and the signal line. When the market is on a bullish trend, the histogram turns green and is above the 0-line. In a bearish market, the histogram is red and below the 0-line.

When the MACD line crosses below the signal line, it means that the market is turning bearish and the histogram is negative. Conversely, the histogram is positive when the MACD crosses above the signal line showing that the market is turning into a bullish trend.

Using MACD indicator to show a change in momentum

The MACD indicator is best used to show the change in momentum between buyers and sellers in the market. Combined with price action analysis, you can comfortably identify entry and exit signals. Identifying trade opportunities is primarily based on the crossover between the MACD and signal line and the behaviour of the MACD histogram.

How to identify buying opportunity using the MACD

When you want to buy an asset, the best period to go long is when the bullish momentum is strong.

Using the MACD, the bullish momentum is strong when the MACD line crosses above the signal line. Note that both these lines must be rising – the steeper the slope, the stronger the momentum. Also, the wider apart they are, the stronger the momentum of the trend.

If the market has been on a downtrend, and the MACD line crosses above the signal line, it is an indicator that the bearish trend is coming to an end. This shows that buyers are exerting upward pressure on the price. In this case, you will notice that the histogram is still below the 0-line but starting to contract and moving upwards towards the 0-line.

An ideal buying opportunity presents when the histogram crosses above the 0-line, and the MACD is trending above the 0-line. When the histogram is green and crosses the 0-line, it shows that the bullish momentum is stronger and expanding in the market.

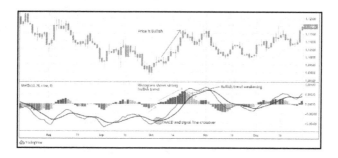

When you notice the MACD and the signal trending closer together above the 0-line, it means that the bullish trend is becoming weaker. This can also be confirmed when the histogram changes colour from green to red. Typically, this would be the ideal point to exit a long trade.

How to identify selling opportunity using the MACD

If the market has been on a bullish trend, when the histogram starts turning red, it means that the price is pulling back. This can be taken as the reversal of the uptrend into a downtrend.

When the red histogram continues to line up is shows that the price is contracting. The ideal opportunity for short selling presents when the histogram is red and below the 0-line together with the MACD. This shows that the downtrend momentum is stronger.

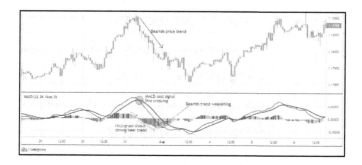

Using the MACD indicator, you can identify exit points for a short trade when the downtrend momentum begins to weaken. This will occur when the histogram starts changing the from red to green. It means that buyers are beginning to exert pressure on the price upwards.

The MACD is best suited as a tool to support whether you are on the right side of the market and not as a standalone signal generator. It would be best if you combined the MACD with the stochastic oscillator and the EMA technical analyses that we have covered in this series. They will help you to identify high probability trading opportunities with low risk.

For example, if you intend on taking a long position, it is best to identify an uptrend in the price action. In this case, you should go long when;

- The price stays above the EMAs
- The stochastic oscillator shows that the selling pressure is absorbed, and
- The MACD is above the 0-line with the histogram has turned green.

Exponential Moving Averages (EMAs)

A price action analysis is essential for every crypto trader. Accurately assessing the price trend of an asset plays an important role in helping traders identify the best trading opportunities. The exponential moving averages (EMAs) help in determining the market trend and momentum.

In this article, we will discuss what EMAs are and how you can use them to identify the optimal trading opportunities.

What is the Exponential Moving Average?

The EMA is a type of moving average which measures the trend of an asset's price over time just like the simple moving average (SMA). However, the EMA assigns more weight to the most recent price points, unlike the SMA, which only averages the price over a particular interval. For this reason, the EMA is more sensitive to price changes than the SMA, which means that it can capture changes in a trend quickly.

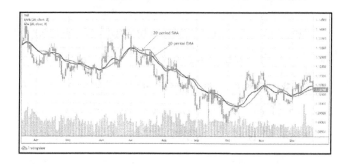

The EMA treats the most recent price as being more relevant than historical price. Thus, as

When computing the EMA, the price applied can be:

- The highest price attained
- The closing price of each period
- The opening price of each period
- The lowest price in each period
- The average of the highest and the lowest in each period
- The average of the highest, lowest, and closing price in each period

- The average of the open, highest, lowest, and closing price in each period

Identifying Entry Points using the EMA

The best way to identify trading opportunities using the EMA is when the markets are trending. By trending markets, we mean when there is a clear pattern of an uptrend or a downtrend. Avoid using the EMA to identify trading opportunities when the market is trending sideways, i.e., when the price is trading in a horizontal channel. In such instances, the price appears to be clustered around the EMA, as shown in the chart below.

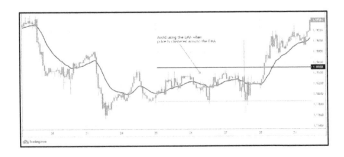

You can adjust the EMA period depending on whether you want to trade a longer- or shorter-term periods. In this analysis, we are going to use a combination of two EMAs to generate trading signals – a 20-period EMA and a 50-period EMA.

Here's the rationale behind this. The 20-period EMA measures the price trend of the past 20 candles while the 50-period EMA measures the trend of the preceding 50 candles. Since the EMA attaches higher weights to the most recent price changes, it means that the 20-period EMA will be responsive to changes in price and thus will be the first one to detect a change in the trend. When the 20-period and the 50-period EMAs are trending in the same direction, it means that the most recent and distant price changes are trending in the same direction.

Note, the steeper the EMAs slope, the stronger the momentum of the trend.

Identifying buy opportunities using the EMA

When you intend on going long, it is best to wait until the EMA shows a clear uptrend. Typically, when the market is on an uptrend, both the 20-period and the 50-period EMAs are sloping upwards.

The EMAs entry confirmation for a long trade occurs when the 20-period EMA crosses and trends above the 50-period EMA. More so, the price of the asset you are trading must be above both the EMAs. This trend confirms that buyers are exerting an upwards pressure on the price.

However, since EMAs can be prone to fake-outs, avoid executing your long trade, the instant a crossover occurs. Instead, wait for a confirmation that the bullish trend will be sustained. How do you get the confirmation? Assuming you are only using the EMAs as your technical indicators, you can get your confirmation by observing the price pullback. Here's how you can use the pullback as a confirmation.

The price of an asset tends to oscillate around the EMA. That means that the price will always be drawn back to the EMA. In this case, if the price pulls back and consolidates around the EMAs and then breaks out again into an uptrend, it means that the sellers are exhausted and could not reverse the uptrend into a downtrend. Thus, we can take this as a confirmation that the bullish trend is strong enough to push the prices further higher.

In this case, execute a long trade when the price breaks and closes above both EMAs.

Identifying short-selling opportunities using the EMA

When using EMA, a short-selling opportunity arises when the 20-period EMA crosses below the 50-period EMA. Furthermore, the price of the asset must be trading below both EMAs. Ensure that there is a clear downtrend formed, with the EMAs sloping downwards.

After the initial crossing of the 20-period EMA below the 50-period EMA, do not rush to sell. Instead, wait for a confirmation that the downtrend is strong enough to push the price lower. Once the price s trending below both EMAs, wait for the pullback. The confirmation for a short position occurs when the price pulls back and consolidates around the EMAs then breaks into a downtrend. This shows that sellers are dominant in the market.

After the pullback, execute the short trade when the price breaks and closes below both EMAs.

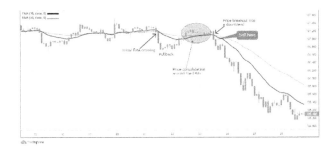

Depending on your trading objectives, you can set a static 'take profit' level, or you can use a trailing stop loss to mark your trade exits.

The EMA is primarily used to establish the trend and momentum of an asset's price. Note that the EMA reacts faster to changes in the trend of the price, which gives you an edge by allowing you to open and close positions when trends are starting to form. However, to avoid falling for possible fake-outs by the EMA, make sure to use pullbacks for trade confirmation. Furthermore, you can use the EMA alongside other price action analysis techniques to establish the optimal entry and exit points.

Bollinger Bands

Bollinger Bands were introduced in the 1980s by John Bollinger. This technical analysis indicator comprises of three lines – a moving average which is in the middle of two lines one above and another below. The upper lines are called bands – upper and lower bands. Before we explain how Bollinger Bands work, we will explain the concept of standard deviation, since it is vital in the functioning of Bollinger Bands.

Standard deviation is used to measure volatility. If you are trading the ETH/BTC pair, the standard deviation of the pair measures how the price of ETH/BTC varies from its mean.

Typically, the middle line in the Bollinger Bands is either simple moving average (SMA) or an exponential moving average (EMA). Let's say for example that you have set your MA at a period of 20, this means that the closing price of the past 20 candles will be averaged. The upper and lower bands are then derived by standard deviations from this MA.

If you set the standard deviation on your Bollinger Bands indicator as 2, the upper band will be +2 standard deviations from the MA while the lower band will be -2 standard deviations from the MA.

Bollinger Bands Trading strategies - Riding the Trend by Using The Bollinger Bands

Typically, when the price of an asset hits the lower Bollinger Band, it is expected that it will rebound. This means that the prevailing market trend will reverse into an uptrend.

This strategy takes advantage of the fact that a trader should go long when the price is lowest. However, before opening a position, please make sure that the general market trend is showing signs of reversal. You may use candlestick patterns to confirm this.

Whenever trading with Bollinger Bands, it is best to use support and resistance levels created by the upper and lower bands. These levels show possible areas of price reversals or breakouts. Thus, it means that with Bollinger Bands, you can trade breakouts or reversals.

The image below shows entry points for a buy-trade using Bollinger Bands. Notice that when going long, the entry position is when the price action is bouncing off the lower Bollinger Band.

Typically, the price of an asset fluctuates between lower and upper Bollinger Bands. In a downtrend, when the price reaches the lower Bollinger Band, it means that that its momentum is slowing down since short sellers are closing their positions and buyers are returning to the market. this can be taken as a precursor to an uptrend. However, if you use this strategy, always wait for the price to bounce off the lower Bollinger Band.

The same strategy employed in taking a long position is used when shorting the market. as shown in the image below, short trades are initiated when the price is bouncing off the upper Bollinger Band. Typically, when there is an uptrend in the market and the price reaches the upper band and bounces off it, it means that buyers are getting exhausted in the market and cannot push the price further. At this point, sellers begin to return to the market pushing the price down. This is shown in the chart below.

Trading the Double Bottom With The Bollinger Bands

This is the simple and most effective trading method. It shows that short sellers tried to push price further downwards but failed- twice. This gives a strong indication that the market is about to turn bullish. This is shown in the image below.

Note that this strategy only works as a reversal strategy. This means that there must be a well-established bearish trend when the double bottoms form.

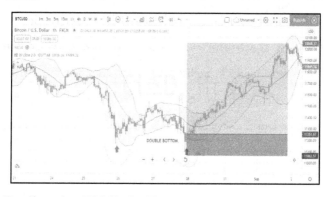

Trading the Middle Bollinger Band

Remember that the middle Bollinger Band is a moving average. By design, moving averages are trend indicators. Thus, when the markets are trending, the middle Bollinger Band can be a string indicator of the trend. When the general market trend is bearish, and the price is bouncing off the MA like a resistance line, it means the market is trending downwards. You can go short. Conversely, When the MA line is sloping upwards, and the price is bouncing off it like a support level, it means that the market is trending upwards. You can go long.

The middles Bollinger Band can also be used as a support or resistance level. If the general market trend is bullish, every now and then there will be short-term pullbacks. These pullbacks will be in the form of short-term downtrends. However, since the long-term trend is bullish, the price reaches the upper band, drops down but doesn't breach below the middle band – it instead bounces off it and continues with the bullish trend.

This shows that sellers could not successfully push the market prices any lower. In this case, whenever you spot an overall bullish trend, you can use these short-term pullbacks to the middle Bollinger Band as entry opportunities to go long.

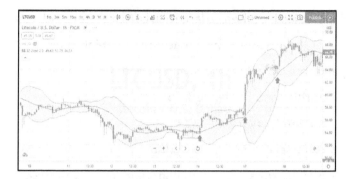

Conversely, when the general market trend is bearish, you can use the short-term bullish pullbacks to the middle band as entry opportunities to go short. In this scenario, these short-term pullbacks occur when the price bounces off the lower Bollinger Band, but the resultant uptrend fails to go beyond the middle band. This shows that buyers failed to push prices higher since sellers dominated the market.

The Engulfing Pattern

The Engulfing pattern is a two-candle technical analysis technique used to identify upcoming reversals of the market trend. The engulfing trading strategy can be used to identify bullish and bearish reversals.

A bullish engulfing pattern indicates a potential reversal of a downtrend into an uptrend. This pattern indicates that there are net buyers in the market and that the price will be pushed to new higher highs. In the bullish engulfing pattern, the fist candle is a bearish one, followed by bullish candle which completely overshadows it.

Conversely, a bearish engulfing pattern indicates the potential reversal of a bullish trend into a downtrend. This means that there are net sellers in the market causing the price to form new lower lows. In the bearish engulfing pattern, the first candle is bullish followed by a bearish candle which completely overshadows it.

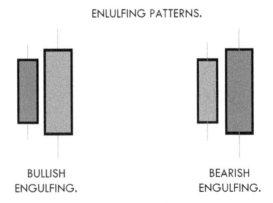

ENLULFING PATTERNS.

BULLISH
ENGULFING.

BEARISH
ENGULFING.

Breakout Trading Using the Engulfing Pattern

Buy Trade

The chart below shows a long trade using the bullish engulfing pattern.

The ideal way of using the bullish engulfing pattern to establish entry position is to combine to with support and resistance. Once you have spotted the formation of the bullish engulfing pattern, you should wait for the confirmation of a bullish trend. this confirmation occurs when the price breaks through the resistance level. This will be your entry point.

You can set a buy stop order or a buy stop limit order at this level. Once the price trends above the resistance level, your buy order will be triggered. This is shown in the chart below.

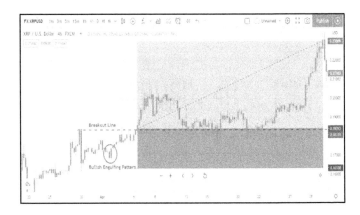

Sell Trade

BCH/USD short trade using the bearish engulfing pattern is shown in the chart below.

As we mentioned earlier, the presence of a bearish engulfing pattern suggests that a bullish trend is coming to an end. When setting up a short sell position, it is best to wait for the confirmation of a bearish trend once the bearish engulfing pattern has formed. This confirmation is given when the price breaks below the support level, as shown in the chart below.

When the price trends below the support level, it shows that sellers are dominating the market hence pushing the price further downwards.

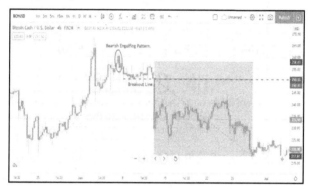

Trading the Bullish Engulfing by Using The Moving Average And RSI

You can also use the engulfing pattern with other technical indicators. Specifically, the moving average and the RSI indicators. These two indicators help to identify the trend and momentum of the price action, hence identifying the optimal entry points.

Bullish Engulfing Pattern

In this example, we have used a combination of the bullish engulfing pattern, the RSI and a 200-period MA. Typically, a bullish trend is identified when the price action is trending above the 200-period MA. Using the RSI, we can identify the start of an uptrend when the indicator is rising from the oversold territory. This shows that buyers are flocking back into the market. the combination of these factors — RSI leaving the oversold territory, price trending above the 200-period MA, and a bullish engulfing pattern — form the ideal entry point for a long trade. Notice how the price forms new higher highs.

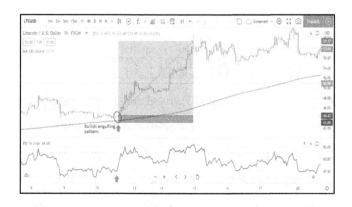

Bearish Engulfing Pattern

The bearish engulfing pattern in BCH/USD pair is represented in the image below

We can also use the same strategy to set up a short position. A bearish trend is observed when the price action is trending below the 200-period MA. Using the RSI, the start of a downtrend is identified when the RSI indicator is leaving the overbought region.

This shows that buyers are exhausted in the market and that there are net sellers in the market, who will push the price further downwards.

An ideal short entry is formed when all these three factors are present on the price chart. i.e., the bearish engulfing pattern has formed, the price action trending below the 200-period MA, and the RSI is leaving the overbought region. Notice in the chart below how the price attains lower lows after the formation of all these three factors.

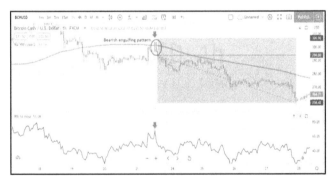

Pros

- This Pattern is easy to use, spot and most effective to trade.

- It is straightforward to master for beginner traders. All they need to do is to identify the pattern visually; there are no calculations needed.

Cons

- The pattern is most useful when the ongoing trend is steady since the pattern shows trend reversal. In a highly volatile market, it becomes difficult to trade with this pattern.

- The second candle of the pattern will be longer sometimes, which can result in a large stop loss to the trader. When it comes to the large stop loss, then take profit should be bigger. The trader is forced to go for larger targets which might be challenging to attain.

TRIX indicator

Jack Huston developed the TRIX indicator in the early 1980s; it is a momentum indicator. The Indicator displays the percentage rate of change to a triple exponentially smoothed moving average.

It is designed to filter out all the insignificant price movements as if they oscillate above and below zero.

By doing this, it also indicates the overbought and oversold regions on the price chart. The positive values of the Indicator indicate the buying momentum, and the negative values indicate the selling momentum. It is a buy signal when the Indicator goes above the zero lines, and a sell signal when the indicator goes below the zero lines.

Be cautious when using the Trix indicator with shorter timeframes. It tends to be more volatile with lower timeframes, and it generates a lot of false signals and on higher timeframes, expect less but accurate signals. Traders mostly use this Indicator to find the divergence between Indicator and price. The bullish and bearish reversals can use to spot the upcoming reversals.

Trading Strategies By Using TRIX indicator overbought and oversold trading

The chart below shows the entry signal for a long trade. As can be seen, the price was in a bearish trend. in this case, when it approached the oversold area, it means the sellers are exhausted, and sooner we can expect buyers to flock back into the market pushing prices into a bullish trend.

When the Indicator gave the reversal at the oversold area, a buy signal is generated. Notice that the price doesn't adopt a bullish trend instantly. This is because buyers and sellers are still playing a "tug of war"; with sellers trying to push prices further downwards and buyers trying to push the prices up. This results in a short-term sideways trending pattern.

Afterwards, the buyers dominate the market and push the price to form a new higher highs.

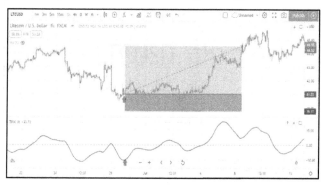

The chart below shows a short sell opportunity using the TRIX indicator. As can be seen the price was in a sustained bullish trend. When the price approached the nearest resistance area, the TRIX indicator also approached the overbought area. This shows that the power of bulls in the market is getting weaker as sellers are coming back into the market.

The price bounced off the resistance level since buyers couldn't sustain the bullish trend any further. The TRIX indicator also started leaving the overbought region. This is an indication that the bullish trend is reversing into a bearish trend. Notice how the price formed new lower lows.

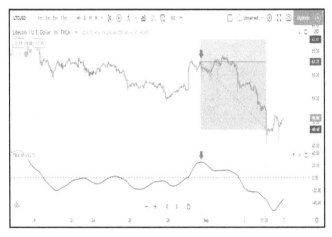

Centerline Strategy

This is the most common and effective strategy which can be used when trading using the TRIX indicator. When the price action goes above the zero lines, it means the trend is gaining momentum, and you can quickly expect the pair to form new higher highs,

So, when the Indicator goes above the centerline, it gives a buying entry signal, and price action steadily adopts an uptrend to form new higher highs. You can place the stop-loss order just below the entry, and exit your position when the TRIX indicator reaches the overbought region. This is shown in the chart below.

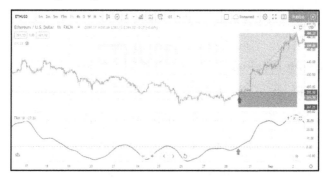

The chart below shows a short sell trade using the TRIX indicator. The price is in an uptrend. When the TRIX goes below the zero line, it is a signal to short the market. After opening the short position, the price trend sideways then adopts a downtrend forming new lower lows.

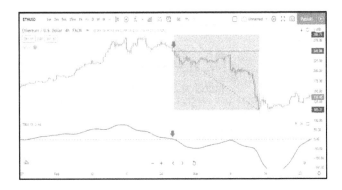

Using Breakout to Trade The Centerline

In this strategy, only trade the center line when the price action breaks the main level. This is preferred due to times the center line fails to provide accurate entry and exit signals.

To filter out any inaccurate signals, use a combination of the centerline with support and resistance levels.

In the chart below, the price is in a bullish trend. notice when the price breaks above the resistance level coincides with when the centerline crosses above the zero line. This presents an accurate long entry as the price formed higher highs.

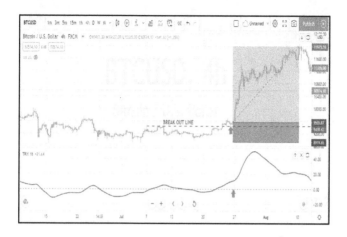

The chart below shows a short sell opportunity using this strategy. The price is in a bearish trend and during the pullback phase, buyers failed to push the price past the resistance level.

Notice that when the price breached the support level, it coincides with when the TRIX indicator crosses the zero line. Subsequently, the price adopts a steady downtrend with the price forming lower lows.

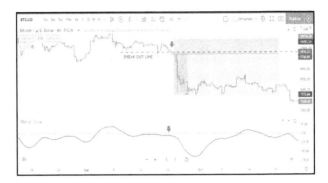

Pros

- TRIX is a trend-following indicator, and is more accurate than other trend -following indicators. This better performance is due to its excellent filtration of market noise and its tendency to lead Indicator in the market.

- TRIX indicator measures the difference between each bar smoothed version of the price information, which makes it the leading Indicator. Hence, it eliminates all the short term price movements that indicate a change in the market direction.

Cons

- TRIX indicator fails to generate any trading signals in the choppy and sideways market. It creates a tight range near the zero lines with these conditions, making it impossible for the traders to identify the signals.

- In a trading market, the indicators linger at the extreme of the overbought and oversold regions for a long. Sometimes, it goes beyond the daily range bounds. This fact makes it difficult to rely on the TRIX indicator when the markets are trending.

Moving Average Trading Strategy

Simple Moving Average Trading Strategy

This is one of the simplest and easy to use trading strategies. It is mostly preferred by day traders since it provides a lot of trading signals intraday. The governing principle of the MA trading strategy is to go long when the price crosses and trends above the MA. Conversely, short the market when the price crosses and trends below the MA. the short term moving averages calculates the average price over a given period. For example, if you have a 20-period MA, it will calculate and plot the average price over the past 20 periods.

Thus, when the price crosses and trends above the MA, it means that the current price is rising faster than the most recent historical average. This shows that the market is adopting a bullish trend. In this case, the signal to go long is generated when the current price crosses above the MA. however, always wait for the candle to close above the MA before going long. Note that when the MA has a steep upward slope it means that the bullish trend is strong.

This is shown in the chart below.

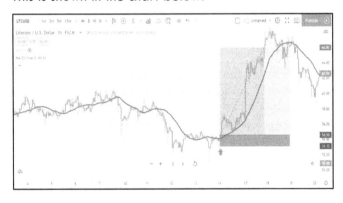

Similarly, when the price crosses and trends below the MA, it means that the current price is dropping faster that the most recent historical average. This shows that the current trend is a bearish one. An opportunity to short the market presents when the price crosses below the MA. this shows that short sellers are dominating the market, pushing the price further downwards. The steeper the slope the stronger the bearish trend.

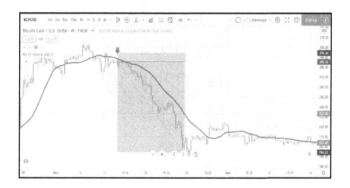

Moving Average Support and Resistance Trading

Moving averages can also be used to determine the support and resistance levels. When you have established the support and resistance levels, it becomes relatively easier to identify entry and exit positions using the MA.

Support levels are formed where the price bounces off the MA. When the price is in a steady uptrend, as it trends further above the MA, there will be series of pullbacks back to the MA. however, since the uptrend has a strong momentum, sellers will fail to push the price action below the MA. The region where the price bounces off the MA line forms the support level. Using these support levels, traders often increase and accumulate long positions whenever there is a pullback. This is shown in the chart below.

Notice that after every pullback to the MA, the price wen on to form higher highs.

The same strategy can be applied to scale your short positions as shown in the chart below.

When the price is in a steady downtrend, it is often accompanied by a series of pullbacks as some short sellers take profit while buyers unsuccessfully attempt

344

to push price beyond the MA line. The resistance level is formed where the price bounces off the MA.

Every time there is a pullback to the MA, you can use it as an opportunity to accumulate your short positions. This is because the downtrend is strong enough that the price cannot break above the resistance level – i.e., the MA line.

One of the most significant advantages of using this strategy is that you can use the MA line as both your entry point and for trailing stop loss.

Double Moving Average Trading Strategy

The chart below shows the set up for using the double MA crypto trading strategy for a buy trade. This strategy involves using two MAs of different periods. The trading signal in this case, both MAs measure the average of the price fluctuation but on different periods. Trade signal are generated when the MAs cross each other.

Here, a bullish signal is generated when the lower-period MA crosses above the higher period MA. this means that the price in the short-term is rising faster than price in the longer-term. It is a clear indication that the market is adopting a bullish trend. Keep in mind that the price action must be trending above both MAs.

More so, in an uptrend, the longer-period MA can be used as the support level. This means that if the price pulls back and drops below the longer period MA, it can be taken as a sign that the bullish trend is reversing into a bearish trend.

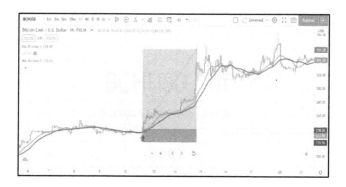

This strategy can also be used to identify short selling signals, as shown in the chart below.

Here, the signal to go short is generated when the shorter period MA crosses and trends below the longer period MA. this shows that the short price trend is dropping faster than the longer average price. It is the initial sign of a bearish trend.

For the short selling signal to be complete, the price action must be trending below both MAs. This shows that the current price is dropping faster than both MAs. In this case, the longer period MA can be used as the resistance level. If the price action pulls back and breaks above the longer period MA, it can be taken as a sign that the bearish trend has reversed into a bullish trend.

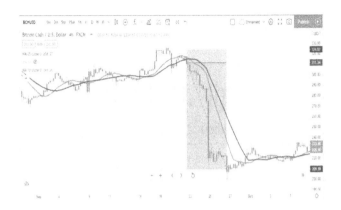

Breakout Trading Strategy Using The 200 Period Moving Average

The 200-day moving average is used to establish a long-term trend. When the price action goes below the MA, it is a sign that the higher timeframes and all the lower timeframes momentum shifted from the selling to buying side. As we have mentioned above, a longer-period MA can be used as either support level or resistance level.

When the price action crosses and trades above the 200-period MA, it's a clear indication that the market has net buyers who are pushing the price, both long-term and short-term higher. As shown in the chart below, once the price crosses the 200-period MA, it subsequently adopts strong bullish trend and forms higher highs.

For short selling using this strategy, the price has to cross the 200-period MA and trend below it. This shows that sellers are dominant in the market, both short-term and long-term pushing prices lower.

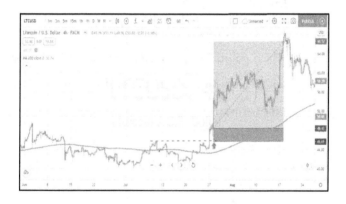

Pros

- A smooth line is given by it, which is less prone to whipsaws of price volatility
- In a trending market, it is sometimes hard to find a support area to enter. The MA solves the problem by giving dynamic support and resistance levels.

- The MA can be used to set trailing stops since they follow the market price

Cons

- It is a lagging indicator. So, it takes a lot of time to generate the trading signal, and as a result, a trader usually took the entry very late.

- MA can be spread out on any timeframe, which could be a problem because the lower timeframe trend can differ from the higher timeframes.

6.7 Best Risk Management Techniques

By definition, the risk is the uncertainty we face about a particular outcome. In crypto trading, the risk is the unknown deviation from expected earnings which presents a downside to trading. However, since this is a known risk, we can use several risk-management measures to limit the potential downside.

Risk management means deploying measures designed to limit a trader's exposure to market risks such as volatility. These techniques help increase earnings from a single trade and help in capital preservation when a trade doesn't go your way.

One of the most convenient risks management techniques involves the use of pending order types. These ensure that your trade is executed at a specific price even when there is extreme volatility. The primary advantage of this technique is that when there is market volatility, executing trading using market orders may result in slippages which are extra costs to the trader. Here are some of the best risk management techniques for a crypto trader:

Do not use excess leverage

Leverage is a credit facility extended to you by your broker, which helps you increase your exposure to a particular asset. For example, if you take leverage of 100x, you will open a position that is 100x the size of your account deposit. Say you have a $1000 deposit in your account. With a leverage of 100x, you can open a position worth $100,000. Note that leverage can only be used when trading derivatives. It significantly increases your potential profits but also makes the downside huge.

In this example, someone with $1000 using the leverage of 100x profits equally from the market as someone with $100000 who isn't using leverage. The risk here is that a slight 1% market shift on the opposite side will wipe out your $1000 account balance. Compared with someone using the leverage of 10x, the market will have to move at least 10% against them for their $1000 account balance to be wiped out. This is the risk of using excessive leverage.

As a risk management technique, traders are often encouraged to use small leverage, or if possible, avoid using leverage.

Capital allocation

The possibility of potential profits often lures novice traders. As the saying goes, the more you invest, the more you earn. While maybe true, the downside is that the more you invest, the more you also stand to lose. But this shouldn't discourage you from trading; it should encourage you to learn proper capital allocation techniques.

As a rule of thumb, traders of all levels of experience are encouraged to allocate not more than 10% of their total account on a single trade. This means that if you have an account balance of $1000, the maximum amount you should risk in a single trade is $100. Some might argue that this caps your potential profit compared to trading with a total of $1000. While this might be true, it also significantly limits your potential losses to just $100. It is better to live to fight another day than go all in, only to crash and burn.

Take Profit orders

These are orders to your broker to close an open position when the price reaches a specified level above the entry-level for a buy order and lower than the entry price for a short position. Take profit orders can also be modified into limit orders.

When you open a long position, it means that you expect the price to go up. As a risk management technique, you should set a take profit level. This is a specific level where you'd want your trade to be closed and for you to take the profits accumulated so far. Typically, the take profit level for a long trade is set above the buying price. Similarly, when you go short, you expect that the price will drop; this means that you set the profit level for a short trade below the selling price.

Stop Loss Orders

As the name suggests, these are designed to limit a trader's downside. They are meant to close out a position if the market trends in the opposite direction. For example, if you open a short position, you hope that the price will drop. Instead, if the currency pair rises, it means that you are accruing losses on your trading account. If these loses continue, your account could be wiped out. However, setting a stop loss order lets you instruct your broker to automatically close your position after the losses in your trading account reach a specific level. Let's see how they are set.

When you open a long position, you expect that the price will rise. But in an adverse scenario where the market doesn't go in your way, it will result in your trading account accruing some loses. Setting a stop loss ensures that your trade will be closed at a specific level, preventing your account from taking further losses. For a long trade, the stop loss is set below the buying price.

Similarly, when you short sell, you expect that the prices will drop. If the market adopts an uptrend, it means that your trading account will accrue losses. Setting a stop loss level ensures the losses you take is capped. For a short sell, the stop loss level is set above the selling price.

Trailing Stop Orders

This order is a modification of the buy stop and the sell-stop orders. Note that the difference with this order is that it isn't used to open positions but for risk management purposes. This order is used to mitigate significant loses in an already opened position. Trailing stop orders are often attached to some pips below the prevailing market price. This means that when the price rises in an open position and your profits accumulate, the trailing stop also rises along with it. When the trend changes and the market adopt a bearish trend, your position will be close when the market price reaches the trailing stop level.

For an open short position, the trailing stop is placed specific points above the market price. As the downtrend continues, the trailing stop will continue moving downwards. This ensures that your profits are secured if the market reverses into a bullish trend. The techniques we have discussed above are implemented after a trade has been executed. However, risk management techniques can also be extended to cover positions that you haven't opened yet. These techniques involve the use of pending orders. Here are some of the most common pending orders you may use:

Session 7
Trading Psychology

7.1 What is Trading Psychology?

Trading psychology is the mental state and the emotions of trader which control their decision-making process. It encompasses the personality traits of a particular individual, including their psyche, behavior, and character, all of which factor in making specific decisions when trading.

It goes without saying that every trader wants to be successful and profit from their trades as much as possible. While many can interpret this as ambition, the line between ambition and greed gets blurry very fast. At its core, trading psychology isn't just about mental fortitude that helps a trader cope with the brutal nature of trading; it helps explain the two biggest emotions in trading – greed and fear.

Greed: as we have mentioned, can often be mistaken for ambition. Say you open a position with your profit target set at 5% of your invested amount. This is a conservative amount by all measures. When your trade hits your target, you feel that you could reap more from this particular trade; so, you shift your profit target to 10%. This is greed. Greed drives many good traders to remain in a position for longer than they should or longer than is necessary.

Greed also drives traders to take large and risky speculative positions using too much leverage. This increases the probability of their account balance is wiped out if the market trends slightly against them. The main distinguishing factor between greed and ambition is that ambition involves making logical trade decisions that do not risk running your account to zero. We will cover more on this in a later section.

Fear: is the opposite of greed when it comes to trading. Fear tends to paralyze traders and either make them avoid getting into a position or closing a position early to avoid losses and taking on a little extra risk. In short, fear makes traders excessively risk averse.

7.2 Importance of Trading Psychology

While most people tend to dismiss trading psychology, it is one of the most important attributes of profitable traders. Perhaps more important than one's knowledge, experience and skills. Understanding trading psychology will help traders achieve the perfect balance of greed and fear. Here are some of the importance of trading psychology.

Helps to understand the fear

In crypto trading, volatility is one of the permanent attributes of the market. As most traders say, volatility is here to stay. In the past two years, crypto trading has become increasingly volatile and markets more unpredictable than ever. Remember, cryptos do have fundamentals like stock or forex trading. In the stock market and forex trading, volatility can be anticipated and explained away using fundamentals. In crypto trading, however, there are no fundamentals to analyze, which means that the market price almost entirely depends on the public's sentiment. And as we covered earlier, sentimental analysis can be pretty hard.

For any trader, the uncertainty and the volatility of the crypto market can take a mental toll and almost always discourage someone from opening a position. To recap, volatility is the unpredictable and rapid fluctuation of the price of a currency pair. High volatility means that a particular currency pair's price fluctuates rapidly and unpredictably during a trading session. Low volatility means that the price has low fluctuations and follows a particular trend.

Here's how fear comes into the picture. Suppose you have done your market analysis accurately so and have determined that the market will drop. The best course of action is to open a short position. Rationally, you know that this would be the best trade. However, looking back a few hours on the chart, you notice high volatility in that particular crypto. You develop a fear that if you go short, volatility might come back and lead to massive losses. Although this is a possibility, you do not know it with certainty. In fact, no one knows with certainty how the markets will trend. But since you are filled with fear, you choose to stay out of the market.

Another scenario plays out when taking profits or stopping losses. Say you have opened a position, and the market is going your way. You obviously have a profit target set, say at 10%. But when your profits reach 5%, you get an irrational fear that the market might reverse the trend and the profits you have made so far will be wiped out. So, you decide to close your trade prematurely and miss out on the potential profits.

Similarly, if you have an open position and the market is seemingly trending against you, you might fear that this trend will persist, which drives you to close your position prematurely to cut loses. With trading psychology, traders get to understand that fear is a natural repose to perceived loses. It helps traders to quantify the perceived threat, which helps them put a limit to their downside. This also helps them understand why such events instill fear in them. Understanding fear enables traders to keep and maintain objectivity with their trades.

True, volatility presents a risk that your trades can run into loses, but if you quantify this risk, you may be able to account for it. This will help put your mind at ease since you know that you will not wipe out your account balance even if the worst comes to happen. This is why using the 'stop loss' function is crucial for crypto traders. It ensures that no matter how volatile the market gets, you will not incur infinite loses. Trades should also use the trailing stop feature to ensure that their profits are protected, even before the price hasn't reached your profit target. This way, when the market reverses its trend, your profits up to that point won't be wiped out.

To recap, a trailing stop for a long trade is often attached to some pips below the prevailing market price. This means that when the price rises in an open position and your profits accumulate, the trailing stop also rises along with it. When the trend changes and the market adopt a bearish trend, your position will be close when the market price reaches the trailing stop level. For an open short position, the trailing stop is placed specific points above the market price. As the downtrend continues, the trailing stop will continue moving downwards. This ensures that your profits are secured if the market reverses into a bullish trend.

Having objectivity eliminates fear, which results in increased profitability for a trader. The trades made will be more and of higher quality since the trader won't have a fear of missing out, which is prevalent among crypto traders. With experience, traders become more adaptable and can easily and effectively manage their fear since they know what to expect from the market.

Overcoming Greed

As we noted earlier, greed drives traders to open over-leveraged positions and stay in a trade for longer than they should. Trading psychology helps to overcome greed since it emphasizes that markets are cyclical and that trends will always change. While everyone's goal is to make as much profit from the market as possible, greedy traders ignore their trading plans and rational thinking. They instead base their decisions on instincts. Understanding trading psychology helps traders understand that trades should be made from strategy and planning.

It also makes them understand the inherent cyclical nature of market trends, which ensures that traders stick to their trading plans.

The knowledge of trading psychology also assuages any notion of 'easy money in trading. Traders who chase easy money do so out of greed and often tend to be over-leveraged, hoping to increase their profits significantly from a single trade. Suffice to say; this is a dangerous practice since a slight market movement against you can wipe out your trading account. It is better to accumulate small profitable trades which add up to significant profits in the long run than risk and lose everything on a single trade.

Helps to avoid snap trading decisions

It has been argued that one of the most admirable qualities of a good trader is the ability to think on their feet and make quick trading decisions. Trading psychology helps a trader prepare a particular mindset and discipline, which helps them stick to their trading plans and avoid getting sucked into FOMO.

FOMO is prevalent in crypto trading, especially since the public's sentiment mostly drives the price of cryptos. Say that a trader has an open position and notices that the public sentiment is about to shift and could potentially result in loses. In this case, the trader faces a challenging task of whether to close out the current position or ride out the market trend's reversal. Trading psychology helps instill the discipline, enabling them to know when to abandon their trading plan and give in to public pressure.

Ensuring flexibility

In trading, nothing is ever set in stone. The market is dynamic and ever evolving. Trading psychology helps you to adapt to the changing times. The crypto market is still nascent, and as DeFi continues to evolve, newer trading instruments will be introduced to the market. This means that a trader should not be rigid but open to using these trading instruments to mitigate risk and enhance profits. Trading psychology helps to understand that diversification is the ultimate goal for risk mitigation; traders shouldn't limit themselves to one class of tradable assets. Take futures and options, for example. Traders exposed to the spot market might use options and futures to mitigate the potential losses from trading in the spot market.

A crypto option is a type of derivative that gives you the right to buy or sell a specified amount of particular crypto in the future for a specific price. This means that if an investor believes that their crypto value will drop in the future, they will use the crypto option to lock in a preferred price for their portfolio. This contract will enable them to sell their portfolio at a specific price even if the future market price is significantly lower than the current price. Similarly, investors can also use options contracts to accumulate their crypto portfolio at a cheaper price.

If they speculate that the price of particular crypto will rise in the future, they use options contracts that allow them to lock in a specific price. This means that when the price of that crypto increases, the options contract allows them to accumulate their portfolio at a cheaper price even when the future market price is significantly higher. The best thing about options contracts is that the holder is not obligated to go through with that transaction.

Ensuring that you set a trading plan and stick with it

Arguably, most of the losses incurred in trading happen due to a lack of a proper trading plan or having a trading plan and not sticking with it. Developing a trading plan means setting guidelines that you will follow when opening and closing positions. These guidelines include the percentage of your capital that will be allocated to a single trade, profit targets, stop loss targets, and which assets to trade. It is considered best practice to trade assets that you are familiar with. This means that you have to do thorough research into your preferred trading instruments. This ensures that you have adequate knowledge of how that particular asset behaves under certain market conditions.

Always remember to only trade amounts that you are comfortable losing. In this case, a single loss will not severely impact your overall portfolio. Also, make sure that when you hit your profit target, close your trade and stay out of the market for a while. This is because you might be tempted to continue trading since you have the notion that you are invincible to loses.

7.3 Healthy Trading Habits

Trading psychology helps you overcome the vices of greed and fear in trading and helps cultivate healthy trading habits. In crypto trading, heathy trading habits include:

Journaling your trade

Trade journaling is one of the most important trading habits a trader can develop. A trade journal works similar to a personal journal; it helps reflect on personal decisions, daily review of trading activities and gives you the benefit of hindsight. This comes in the form of post-trade analysis; you will see patterns more vividly and tweak some of your trading strategies, which will help you become more profitable.

Typically, a trade journal is the record of all your trades in chronological order. While trading journals differ, almost all of them have basic components, which include the time when you opened and closed a trade; entry and exit price of the asset traded; the size of the position; the direction of the trade – long or short; and the result of the trade i.e., whether the trade was profitable or not, and by how much. You may also customize your trading journal to include a personal review of each trade. These include the rationale behind each trade; the types of trade order you used; personal views regarding the general trend of the market; personal assessment of the trade, i.e., whether you stuck to the trading plan or made mistakes during the trade. This incorporates a retrospective element to your journals which help you reflect on your trading habits.

A trading journal will help you monitor your trading progress over an extended period to establish your trading strategy profitable in the long run. Obviously, no single trading strategy is 100% profitable; what matters is that the number of winning trades should be more than those of the losing ones. The only way you get to see this is by monitoring your trades in the long-term with the trading journal. It also helps you improve your trading strategies since you can tweak the strategy as time goes by. This is done by identifying the strengths and weaknesses of your strategies.

Making a trading plan

One of the most talked-about characters of successful traders is that they have a trading plan. A trading plan is best described as a personal trading guide that includes your financial goals, risk management techniques you will employ in different scenarios, and your preferred assets. Always ensure to have a well-researched trading plan which is personalized. To create a good trading plan, you need to ask yourself these questions:

- Why do you want to trade, and what type of trader do you want to be?
- How much capital are you willing to invest?
- How much time do you wish to spend trading?
- Do you accept the risks that are involved in trading?

Remember that your trading plan should be grounded on logical research, have well-established entry and exit points, and proper risk management techniques.

When developing your trading plan, you must remember that this is not a rigid plan; you should be open to modifying it. However, you should also have your favorite trading strategies that you will always stick to. It is easier to be accountable when using a few strategies in your trades than implementing several strategies. This would make your trades seem random, and it would be difficult for you to assess your progress. More so, it also helps you to remain consistent.

Always practice your trading strategy in a demo account

Being a profitable trader is a skill that is honed over a long period. To gain mastery of the markets, you have must practice first trading in a demo account. A demo account provides you with a real trading experience without you having to risk your capital. Here, you can practice different trading strategies, and conduct thorough back tests to determine which ones will be profitable in the long run. After you are confident that you have a winning strategy, you may want to try trading with a real account using a small capital first. This will help you cope with the mental strain involved when trading using real money.

Don't dismiss losing trades

Most traders would want to shrug off the losing trades. This is probably not a good idea. In finance, stories of failures have a lot teach than stories of success. A winning trade could have performed well because you have a perfect trading strategy or purely out of luck. If you open trades randomly, without doing any market research or analysis, the chances are that you will have at least a few winning trades. There isn't much to learn from profitable trades; all you leant is that your trading strategy works, or you got lucky.

Consider the opposite. Say you have done thorough back tests on your trading strategy, you have done impeccable market and technical analysis, but when you open a trade, it turns out to be a losing trade. On the off chance that with was just back luck, you have a lot to learn. Such losing trades will trigger introspection on your part; you will tear apart your strategy t find out why it failed, you will look for evidence to explain away the loss. This is how growth happens in trading. It will help you discover things about the market or even about you as a trader. The point is, embracing losing trades is a healthy trading habit.

Learn from successful traders

What has proven to under certain conditions will always work under those conditions. This is why it is crucial to learn from successful traders. Those who have constantly registered profits. In the age of the internet, a few online searches, and you will find success stories. Try to learn, but only the verifiable stuff. There are several free online courses and video tutorials that will help you master trading strategies and techniques. However, as we mentioned earlier, don't dive in headfirst. Always test these strategies in demo accounts to see if they work.

Remember that trading is a continually evolving field; even experienced traders are always on the learning curve.

Always use stop loses and trailing stops

This is the one point we cannot emphasize enough. It is one of the most underrated aspects of healthy trading habits. Stop-loss levels help ensure that your downside is finite and limited if the market goes against you. They also prevent you from freaking out and closing your trades prematurely. More so, if you do not set a stop loss level and choose to exit a trade manually, market slippages may still compound the losses you incur from a bad trade.

This is how to stop loss works. For example, if you open a short position, you hope that the price will drop. Instead, if the currency pair rises, it means that you are accruing losses on your trading account. If these loses continue, your account could be wiped out. Setting a stop loss order lets you instruct your broker to automatically close your position after the losses in your trading account reach a specific level.

On the other hand, trailing stop helps to secure the profits you have earned up to a certain period. For example, if the market trends your way for some time, your trade is profitable, but if the trend reverses before the price hits your take profit level, you stand to lose all the profits accumulated up to that point. This is where the trailing stop comes in.

Remember that trailing stop orders are often attached to some pips below the prevailing market price for a long trade. This means that when the price rises in an open position and your profits accumulate, the trailing stop also rises along with it. When the trend changes and the market adopts a bearish trend, your position will be close when the market price reaches the trailing stop level. For an open short position, the trailing stop is placed specific points above the market price. As the downtrend continues, the trailing stop will continue moving downwards. This ensures that your profits are secured if the market reverses into a bullish trend.

Pay attention to market sentiment

Crypto trading is fundamentally different from stock or forex trading since a crypto trader cannot perform fundamental analysis on particular crypto and determine whether to buy or sell. The market sentiment almost entirely drives the crypto market. The inherent value of cryptos is tied to what other people are willing to pay for them. This fact makes sentimental analysis invaluable to crypto traders. Although sentimental analysis can be convoluted, it can be simplified by following crypto news websites and most financial news channels. Whenever there is a significant movement in the crypto market, the news headlines will capture it.

To recap, sentimental analysis of cryptos is similar to fundamental analysis, only that it involves a more personal and subjective analysis of the public's opinion. In the long run, crypto investors might be unaffected by sentimental analysis. Crypto traders are the most impacted by the public's sentiment regarding particular crypto. You can use this information to trade the market. Remember that reading accurately into the public sentiment in the crypto market is probably the only thing standing between you and profitable trade.

7.4 How Not to Sabotage Your trading?

Even expert traders can sometimes sabotage their trading. It may not be a deliberate act, but our subconscious mind can sometimes drive us into inexplicable sabotage. Whether you are an experienced professional trader managing a billion-dollar fund, or a novice trader with just a few hundred dollars, here are some ways to not sabotage your trading.

Stick to the plan!

We have mentioned the trading plan throughout this session. That is because it plays a crucial role in determining your long-term profitability. After all, isn't long-term profitability the end goal here? There are several ways in which not sticking to your trading plan can prove disastrous. Here is a couple of scenarios.

Firstly, say you have opened your trade and have already set your stop loss and take profit levels. This means that you can take a nap and let the trade be.

However, if the market seems to be going against you, and you are convinced that you made the wrong trade, you will be tempted to close out that trade and open another trade in the opposite direction. This is ill-advised. You have to remember that you already set your stop loss levels and that as per your trading plan, you can afford to lose this trade since the loss won't significantly impact your account balance.

Secondly, when you have achieved your profit target and notice that the market is still trending in your direction, do not be tempted to open another similar trade or adjust your TP levels. This is a classic FOMO trait, and it may backfire, so why risk it?

Do not second-guess yourself
In trading, even the most successful traders know that there is no perfect trade of a perfect strategy. Especially when it comes to crypto trading, where the market is governed by human sentiment, with this in mind, once you have conducted your market research and are ready to open a trade, avoid any second thoughts which might paralyze your trading. If possible, train yourself to be cold and calculating

when it comes to trading. Provided you have the data, stick to it.

Also, do not regret the wrong trades. No one has a perfect trading record. We all have wins and losses under our belts. Sometimes it may be that we made mistakes or that the trading strategies were ill-suited. But second-guessing may cause you to throw out your entire trading system. In the end, this could sabotage your trading or, worse, result in inconsistency.

Commit yourself to learn

We have mentioned this before; the crypto market is still nascent and continually evolving. This means that even if you are an experienced trader now, chances are, you do not know everything there is to know about trading. The arrogance of assuming that you are a pro and have nothing more to learn may severely sabotage your trading. Always be open to continue evolving with the market.

Avoid over-leveraging

Whenever you are trading, remember that the market is cyclical. If you are over-leveraged, a slight market movement against you could wipe out your trading account before the desired trend develops in the market.

Session 8
Crypto Lending Making Passive Income with Cryptos

8.1 What is Crypto Lending & How Does It Work?

Crypto lending involves giving out your cryptos as loans. Lending allows those HODLing cryptos to earn interest on their portfolio. It also serves to increase liquidity in the crypto market by freeing up cryptos held in cold storages. Crypto lending can occur on centralized or decentralized platforms.

How does crypto lending work?

Centralized crypto lending platforms operate similar to the traditional banking system. These platforms decide who is eligible for a crypto loan and the interest rate to be charged. These platforms adhere to strict know your customer (KYC) protocols. This means that your cryptos will only be lent out only to trustworthy borrowers, and the interest earned solely depends on the changes in supply and demand.

Decentralized crypto lending platforms use smart contracts to issue and manage crypto loans autonomously. Using smart contracts, anyone can originate a crypto loan and lend to anyone with no KYC needed.

Smart contracts allow lenders to pool their cryptos together and automatically distributes the loans to borrowers. It has the terms of these loans codified into the contract, which also autonomously distributes interest to the lenders. Typically, borrowers deposit funds to a smart contract, often in fiat, for more than the amount of crypto loan they wish to take. This is called collateralization, and some platforms require borrowers to collateralize their loans by a minimum of 150%.

The collateral is used by smart contract to guarantee that crypto lenders do not lose their money due to market volatility. The smart contract automatically begins liquidating the collateral if the value of the loan goes beyond a specified percentage.

8.2 Best Crypto Lending Platforms

1. Venus

Venus is a decentralized crypto exchange (DEX) and one of the top lending platforms. Launched in November 2020, Venus uses Binance Smart Chain to tokenize crypto assets. It is touted as a decentralized marketplace for borrowers and lenders with borderless stablecoins.

Venus Liquidity

As of this publication, Venus had an average 24-hour turnover of $101.65 billion. According to Coinbase, this accounts for about 99.88% market share of decentralized lending platforms. This means that users can access instant liquidity.

Venus Collateral

Users who want to borrow on Venus must collateralize their loans but can only borrow the equivalent of 75% of their collateral. Liquidation will be triggered if the value of your collateral drops below 75%.

Note that the collateral must be in crypto since Venus Exchange doesn't accept deposits in fiat currency.

Venus Fees and Interest

There are no 'taker' or 'maker' fees applicable on Venus, i.e., no trading fee is incurred on Venus, only network fee. Although the network fee charged varies daily, it is well below the global industry average. Thanks to the Binance, Smart Chain transactions are fast, and fees are low.

Lenders earn a compounded interest rate annually (APY) paid per block. This ranges from 1.13% to 13.41%. The interest earned is determined by the protocol in a curve yield which is automated based on the demand for the particular crypto being borrowed.

Venus Supported Cryptos

Venus uses a synthetic stablecoin (VAI) which is collateralized by various stablecoins and cryptos. The Venus Protocol enables users to mint VAI. When users supply their crypto for lending, receive a vToken which will be used to redeem the collateral supplied by borrowers. For example, if you supplied BTC for lending, you will receive vBTC to either transfer into cold storages that support Binance Smart Chain or hedge against other cryptos.

Venus supports 17 cryptos; ADA, BETH, FIL, DAI, LINK, DOT, BCH, XRP, LTC, ETH, BTCB, BNB, BUSD, USDT, USDC, XVS, and SXP.

2. Compound

Compound is decentralized lending exchanged founded in May 2019. Users on the platform can supply their cryptos in return for a synthesized token which they can use to redeem their cryptos at any time. For example, if you supply ETH, you receive cETH, which you can convert to BTC at any time.

Compound's Liquidity and Supported Cryptos

As of this writing, Compound had a 24-hour trading volume of $101.17 billion. The platform supports nine cryptos, including; DAI, USDC, WBTC, ETH, USDT, UNI, COMP, BAT, and ZRX.

Compound doesn't support fiat currencies. Any deposits and withdrawals must be in crypto.

Compound's Fees and Interest

Compound exchange doesn't charge any fee on transactions. The Compound protocol is free to use and openly accessible to anyone.

The interest received by lenders and paid by borrowers is determined by an algorithm based on the market supply and demand for specified crypto. There is no minimum lending or borrowing amount, and the lender can earn interest about every 15 seconds, or they may choose to compound the interests for as long as they wish. Note that borrowers and lenders interact directly with the smart contracts, and there are no counterparty negotiations since everything is automated.

For lenders, the annual percentage yield (APY) differs depending on the crypto: 5.92% for DAI, USDC 2.86%, WBTC 0.18%, ETH 0.19%, USDT 2.47%, UNI 0.29%, and 0.83% for ZRX. For borrowers it's; 8.42% for DAI, 3.98% USDC, 3.83% WBTC, ETH 2.89%, USDT 3.7%, UNI 4.92%, and ZRX 7.02%.

3. AAVE

Originally known as ETHLend, AAVE was launched in November 2017. It is a decentralized cryptocurrency lending platform and the first DeFi lending protocol. With AAVE, crypto lenders deposit their funds into a pool that borrowers can access. Lenders are issued with aTokens that allow them to collect interest and withdraw their cryptos any time they wish to.

AAVE Liquidity and Supported cryptos

As of this publication, AAVE had liquidity of about $5.4 billion. The platform supports 24 cryptos: AAVE, BAL, BAT, BUSD, CRV, DAI, ENJ, GUSD, KNC, LINK, MANA, MKR, REN, SNX, sUSD, TUSD, UNI, USDC, USDT, WBTC, WETH, XSUSHI, YFI, and ZRX.

However, borrowers can only access DAI, USDT, TUSD, USDC, KNC, MKR, WETH, BAT, MANA, WBTC, ZRX, LINK, REN, and ENJ.

AAVE Fees and Interest

Borrowers who take loans denominated by AAVE do not incur platform fees. AAVE offers overcollateralized loans between 50% to 75%.

However, the platform is introducing under-collateralized loans, which could be the first step towards non-collateralized loans. The non-collateralized loans are called flash loans but only available to developers due to the technical expertise required. With these loans, liquidity must be returned to the protocol within one block transaction.

AAVE has variable and stable rates for borrowers. Stable rates are fixed in the short term but can be adjusted in the long-term depending on the market conditions. Adjusting the stable rate only happens when the average borrow rate falls below 25% while the utilization rate goes above 95%.

During this writing, lenders on AAVE could receive APY of up to 15.4%, depending on the crypto deposited. With variable annual percentage rate (APR), borrowers incur between 0.03% up to 31.54%, while with stable APR, they incur between 0.18% to 36.54%.

4. BlockFi

BlockFi is a centralized crypto lending platform launched in August 2017 and is considered the best crypto lending platform for beginners. Since it's headquartered in the US, it complies with strict federal laws and KYC and AMLpolicies. It is also a CME liquidity provider for bitcoin futures and options block.

BlockFi supported cryptos

BlockFi supports ten cryptos: BTC, ETH, LTC, USDC, GUSD, LINK, USDT, BUSD, PAXG, and PAX.

Users can deposit their cryptos with BlockFi and receive a loan denominated in US Dollars. The loans are overcollateralized by at least 50%. That means if you deposit, say, BTC worth $1000, you are eligible for a USD denominated loan worth $500.

BlockFi Fees and Interest

If you deposit your cryptos with BlockFi Interest Account (BIA), you are eligible to earn interest at the beginning of every month, which can be compounded to increase the APY.

Deposits of up to 2.5 BTC earns an APY of 6% while >2.5 BTC earns a 3% APY. Altcoins have no deposit thresholds. LINK deposits attract an APY of 5.5%, ETH 5.25%, LTC 6.5%, USDC 8.6%, GUSD 8.6%, PAX 8.6%, PAXG 5%, USDT 9.3%, and BUSD 8.6%.

The interest in crypto-backed loans depends on the collateral and the loan-to-value (LTV) ratio. LTV of 50% attracts a 9.75% interest rate, 35% LTV attracts a 7.9% interest rate, and a 20% LTV attracts a 4.5% interest rate. Note that all loans have an origination fee of 2%.

BlockFi allows one free crypto withdrawal and one free stablecoin withdrawal per calendar month. Subsequent withdrawals during that month attract withdrawal fees. More so, there is a 7-day withdrawal limit for every account.

5. Celsius Network

Celsius Network is a decentralized person-to-person lending platform launched in June 2017. It was built around the Celsius crypto wallet, allowing users to use the cryptos sored in their wallets as collateral for loans. To date, Celsius Network has processed about

$8.2 billion worth of loans for over half a million users.

Celsius Network supported cryptos

Celsius Network is considered the best crypto lending platform in terms of the variety of cryptos supported. It supports 36 different cryptos, including; ETH, CEL, BTC, SNX, MATIC, BNT, PAX, BUSD, TCAD, THKD, TAUD, USDT, DAI, USDC, TGBP, GUSD, TUSD, AAVE, UMA, XAUT, DASH, PAXG, COMP, LINK, BCH, EOS, LTC, BAT, ZRX, XLM, ETC, KNC, UNI, XRP, ZEC, MANA, BSV, and OMG.

To start earning interest on Celsius Network, one only needs to create a Celsius wallet, deposit cryptos, and interest will start accruing immediately. However, the interest is calculated weekly and can be compounded.

Celsius Network Fees and Interest

Users can earn interest of up to 17.78% annually by simply depositing their cryptos on Celsius Network. The interest is calculated weekly but can be compounded for as long as the user chooses. You can also withdraw the principal and your interest at any time. When you deposit your cryptos, they are converted to CEL tokens. The CEL tokens can be used to receive and pay interest, send and receive payments, and be staked to earn higher interest rates.

Users on Celsius Network are classified into four tiers; Bronze, Silver, Gold, and Platinum. **Bronze Tier**: Users have 5 to 10% of their crypto portfolio held as CEL tokens. They are entitled to 5% interest payments and a loan discount of 5%.

Silver Tier: 10 to 15% of the portfolio is held in CEL tokens. Users receive 10% interest and a 10% discount on loans

Gold Tier: 15% to 20% of the portfolio is held in CEL tokens. Users receive 20% interest and a 20% loan discount.

Platinum Tier: 20% to 100% of the portfolio is held in CEL tokens. Users receive a 30% interest and a 20% loan discount.

Users on Celsius Network do not incur any fees — there are no loan origination fees, withdrawal fees, deposit fees, default fees, nor early termination fees.

Borrowing on Celsius Network attracts interest rates as low as 1% APR. Taking CEL denominated loans attracts interest rates of as low as 0.7% APR. The interest payable on a loan varies depending on the supply and demand of a particular currency, duration of the loan, and the loan to value (LTV) ratio, ranging from 20% to 50%.

Conveniently, Celsius Network has a calculator for both loan and earnings to calculate the potential cost and rewards, respectively.

6. Nexo

Nexo is a centralized crypto lending platform launched in 2018. The platform has processed more than $1.8 billion for more than a million users in 200 countries globally. Nexo has insured user deposits for up to $350 million; this is in partnership with Ledger Vault and BitGo. It plans to increase its insurance coverage to over $1 billion in 2021.

Nexo supported cryptos

Nexo supports 17 cryptos, including; USDT, USDC, PAX, TUSD, DAI, HUSD, BTC, ETH, XRP, BCH, LTC, BNB, EOS, LINK, XLM, TRX, and PAXG.

Nexo accepts fiat currencies, and users can earn interest in EUR, GBP, and USD. Borrowers also have access to 40 fiat currencies.

Nexo Fees and Interest

Lenders can earn between 8% and 10% APY by depositing their crypto with Nexo. For EUR, GBP, and USD, they earn 10% APY. However, if lenders have at least 10% of their holding in NEXO, the platform's native token, they are eligible to receive an extra 2% in interest.

There are no stringent KYC policies for one to be eligible for a loan with Nexo. You can receive instant cash loans in 40 fiat currencies, USDC, or USDT with no credit checks. However, only these cryptos are accepted as collateral with Nexo: BTC, ETH, XRP, LTC, XLM, BCH, EOS, PAXG, NEXO, and BNB. The loan attracts interest rates of as low as 5.9% APR.

Final Words

We really hope you found this book educational and informative. Although there is so much more to cover, we think this book is comprehensive enough for both novices and intermediate crypto traders. The crux here is to read, reread and apply all the concepts discussed in this book to master them. Just vaguely going through them won't help much. Also, please make sure to bast test these strategies on a demo account before applying them on the live markets. You can actually filter and pick the ones that are working for you and discard the others.

Wishing you all the best! Cheers!

CPSIA information can be obtained
at www.ICGtesting.com
Printed in the USA
BVHW090110161221
624023BV00010B/1009